Failing Gloriously and Other Essays

by Shawn Graham

with an introduction
by Eric C. Kansa

and an afterword
by Neha Gupta

The Digital Press at the University of North Dakota
Grand Forks, ND

2019. The Digital Press at the University of North Dakota

Unless otherwise indicated, all contributions to this volume appear under a Creative Commons Attribution 4.0 License:
https://creativecommons.org/licenses/by/4.0/legalcode

Library of Congress Control Number: 2019953926

ISBN-13: 978-1-7328410-6-2 (ebook)
ISBN-13: 978-1-7328410-8-6 (Paperback)

*Failing Gloriously
and
Other Essays*

This volume is dedicated firstly to the students in the welding program at Pontiac High in Shawville, Quebec, and secondly to those who gave me the benefit of the doubt when things went sideways.

Contents

Foreword by Eric C. Kansa i
Introduction v

Failing Gloriously 1

Part One: Unlearning 15
The First Time 17
On Teaching High School 25
The Smoking Crater 31
Papers, Please 35

Part Two: Getting Over Myself 47
The Man at the Door 49
Mashed Potatoes 53
The Wake 57
Rock of Ages 61

Part Three: Fits and Starts and Fumbles 65
How I Lost the Crowd 71
Research Witchcraft 81
Horses to Water 87
Letter to a Young Scholar 89
I Don't Know How to Do This 95

Part Four: Possibilities 99
What Is This Thing? 101
Rehashing Archaeology 105
Small Acts of Disruption 111
Some Assembly Required 117

Conclusion: To Walk in the Air 127

Afterword by Neha Gupta 131

Reference 135
About the authors 139

Forward
Eric C. Kansa

Shawn chose the word "failing" as a unifying theme to these essays. Failure, self-doubt, anxiety, imposter syndrome, exhaustion, and disappointment seem commonplace in contemporary academic settings. This sort of disaffection has emerged from the shadows to see public expression as a whole genre of "quit lit" literature. While sometimes colored by melancholy, these essays aren't quit lit. They're about empathy and compassion—empathy for students, friends, family, and colleagues.

Shawn tries to build that empathy by emphasizing how his work is not the work of solitary scholarly "genius." His style of work is the circuitous product of endless and shockingly tenacious tinkering, experimentation, and eclectic curiosity. As alluded to by the book's title, many of these essays recount projects that sometimes go wrong. Humble brag disclosure: my own collaboration with Shawn in running a prize competition gets its own failures dissected as well. Another humble brag: one of my first interactions with Shawn came about after he inadvertently took down Open Context by "enthusiastically" consuming our API (software interface). He apologized in a delightfully Canadian manner.

Shawn, as do I, benefits from structural advantages to tinker and get things wrong survivably. He tries to grapple with what, if anything, his experiences in failure and doubt can mean to colleagues and students who navigate social media and academia without the benefit of unearned structural privileges. He argues that he has a sort of ethical obligation "to fail publicly" or even "gloriously" (which sounds almost Homeric) in order to make it safer for others without these advantages to fail.

I'm not sure that recounting embarrassing anecdotes of lost data, confused students, or disinterest in prize competitions (sigh!) will help make Shawn's workstyle of survivable failure necessarily more inclusive. After all, Silicon Valley often celebrates the "heroic failure" of brave entrepreneurs (well-connected white men with access to seed capital) who take risks (mainly with other people's money and livelihoods). Technologists have only rarely reflected on exactly who gets the privilege to tinker and break things and who suffers the collateral damage of that play. In the wake of revelations about how the MIT Media Lab's (male) leadership networked with Jeffry Epstein, a financier, pedophile, and human-trafficker, the cruel and pervasive sexism under the glamour of the "boys and their (digital) toys" has come into stark focus. The technology sector's "move fast and break things" mentality is, in the words of Dana Boyd, "an abomination if your goal is to create a healthy society."[1]

Instead of celebrating failure, I think Shawn's more important contributions center on situating his own experiences with trial and error within a larger context of how risk means very different things to different people in the research community. He uses his discussion of failure to highlight undercurrents of gendered and racial violence that make failure far more dangerous and costly for many classes of people. For some, a daring act can mean driving to a mainly white

---

[1] See Dana Boyd's acceptance speech for an award from the Electronic Frontier Foundation in recognition of her activism on September 11, 2019, one week after Joi Ito resigned as director of the MIT Media Lab: https://medium.com/@zephoria/facing-the-great-reckoning-head-on-8fe434e10630

institution and exposing oneself to racially targeted violence by the police. For others, daring may involve facing workplaces that threaten belittlement or even sexual assault.

While I doubt that recounting examples of failure itself will make the research community more inclusive, the more lasting and significant contribution of these essays really center on Shawn's powerful expressions of humility and empathy. In his discussion of failure, he appropriately cites and engages with the voices and contributions of scholars like Katherine Cook, Lorna Richardson, Bethany Nowviskie, Kisha Supernant, and many others. His essays and his thoughtful citations demonstrate the centrality of compassion in research, teaching, and learning. Thus, these essays offer far more than amusing anecdotes about various goof-ups (though some are indeed hilarious). They demonstrate how love, compassion, and empathy enrich scholarship. These essays help bring about the kinds of "Generous Thinking"[2] that Kathleen Fitzpatrick envisions for a more humane and just future.

---

[2] See: https://kfitz.info/generous-thinking-the-university-and-the-public-good/

Introduction

I fell down the stairs this morning. Took a step, put my foot out into the air, and fell.

As metaphors go, that's a pretty good one.

Finishing grad school was similar. I took a step out into the air, confident that there'd be something *there* to put my foot on. And I tumbled. Lord, how I tumbled. For eight years I tumbled. I ended up living in a motel next to the highway (one of *those* kinds of places) for a while, eventually having to move back into my parents' spare room. It took a long time to climb back from that place. It was not a good place mentally, emotionally, financially, or physically. In a certain genre of book, I would tell you that the climb out was due entirely to my own bootstrapped hard work and good sense, that my natural ability shone through and won the day. But it didn't really happen like that.

This is a book about being an imposter, about recovery and failing gloriously, about learning the advantages of being an imposter the hard way. It is not a recipe book. It is not a self-help book. It is a kind of academic autobiography, following the emergence and appearance of one loose thread in the larger fabric of my career. We can only see this loose thread in retrospect; I've identified it as "failing gloriously." In truth, the experiences that shape and bring us to particular points in our careers are not as tightly coupled as autobiography would suggest. Please don't see this book as motivational; take it instead as one perspective on trying to have a scholarly life in a new academic landscape. My aim in writing this book is that it might make someone else's journey a little less hard, that it might provide cover for someone else to fail gloriously. That you might take a step in the air . . . and fly.

I graduated in 2002 from Reading University in the UK. I spent a year or so after graduation living out of my backpack, trying to string together academic jobs here and there, hoping that each one would be my big break. Hope can be a terrible thing. When a university has you working as an adjunct/sessional, why would they ever offer more? You're trapped. Or at least, I felt trapped, and so I returned home to Canada, becoming the Ottawa Valley's only expert in stamped Roman brick from the first to third centuries. I returned home, my tail between my legs. *If you were any good, you wouldn't be here.*

I had been the guy for whom school had always come easily. I did everything I was supposed to do, jumping the hurdles and progressing through a PhD program. And yet here I was: *if you were any good, why didn't you make it over there?* Coming home felt like humiliation. Even worse, I didn't *belong* at home, not anymore. I'd been away too long, and rightly or wrongly, I didn't fit in. There was no work for me. There was no social framework to fit into. Shawn-who'd-gone-away-and-now-is-unemployed-serves-him-right. I was an imposter, a fraud. I turned to substitute teaching at the local high school, the school where I'd been a student only a decade earlier. But then I felt like a professional imposter, like I was only stepping into someone else's class, someone else's context, knowing that no matter what I did, I was only a temporary caretaker for someone else's work.

My substitute teaching lasted for one and a half academic years, but during that time I discovered a network that offered distance high school education for remote regions, and I found work teaching one or two classes that way. After a brief hiatus back in the world of academia as a postdoctoral student, I was able to string together online teaching jobs at an American for-profit university, as well as hustle for research contracts at various organizations around Ontario.

By that point, I'd quite given up on my naive undergraduate "plan" (which had always been rather fuzzy) of being an archaeologist. I started blogging as a way of performing to myself that identity as an archaeologist that I'd largely let go of as a viable way of life. So I'd blog; I'd play with what archaeological data I could find online, and I would try things. It didn't matter that no one read what I was writing. Online, nobody knew you weren't a *real* archaeologist.

In a different universe, that would have been the end of it. I certainly wouldn't be sitting here putting together this book in a university library coffee shop. A bit of serendipity led to me taking one last stab at an academic job *just* as my role at the online university was being terminated. It turned out that my experiences in online education, and my quiet blogging for my own entertainment, had positioned me at the right moment, in the right space, for this thing called "digital humanities."

Between 2002 and 2010 I had two interviews for full-time academic work. Once was as a Roman archaeologist, the second was as a digital humanist. One was for something I had trained to be, the other was for something I didn't know existed. That I got the second job through what feels like a lot of luck and timing means that I wrestle every day with the sheer arbitrariness of it all. Where is the fairness in any of this?

This book is not a hymn of praise to the virtues of hard work. This is not anti-quit-lit, keep-on-trying-you'll-get-that-academic-job-anyway. I'm telling you this just to say: I *know* I'm an imposter. I was a white guy on the internet in the mid-aughts and benefited from that privilege in ways it took me years to appreciate. No one ever attacked me for admitting ignorance online. No one ever attacked me for trying something different online. It is presumptuous to write this small volume, because I know that there are so many people out there who are more deserving of your time, who would have made better digital humanists had they been given the chance. *Imposter. Who do you think you are?*

That question does no one any good. A better question is: *Now that you've benefited from that privilege, what have you done with it?* This volume is my attempt at figuring that out. I was introduced recently as a senior figure in the field, and the shock of that moment completely derailed me. Why should anyone listen to me, this imposter who worries every day that this too will be taken away? I had to become something else just to get the job. I'm a long way away from the archaeology of the first- and second-century Roman construction industry where I began. Trying to figure out what I am now has marked my *next* eight years. What have I done with this position? What have I done *for you*?

Well . . . Maybe I've learned how to fail gloriously? And maybe that's made some space for you to try something out, to use that imposter syndrome to good effect.

Failing Gloriously is a personal collection of stories, reflections, triumphs, and failures, written from 2003 to 2018. It is not an academic book, but a book about trying to find my way as an academic. The tone and voice of the pieces collected here shift registers, but it is definitely *my* voice, sometimes scholarly, often not. Most of the pieces in this collection began life as blog posts through which I would think out loud, think in public, and fail productively. I have a complicated relationship with "failure" and "productive failing." Learning to fail productively is not without risk and pain. It's not easy. It's not a gimmick. Some of the stories I share here *hurt*. To fail *gloriously* is to share and use the productive fail to offer others a shortcut. To fail gloriously is to embrace the freedom that being an imposter can give, to tinker, to break things, to imagine how things could be different, and to make it safe for others to do the same.

I'm a white tenured professor, working primarily on the internet. Your productive failure is going to look very different from mine, because it is not safe for everyone to do what I did. Your glorious failures do not have to be public. But I think, if I'm to be of any use in this world, mine have to be. Because of the privileges I have been afforded, through my public failures I hope to offer other people cover to explore the potential to use their own imposter syndrome in ways that are productive for them in their own situations. Because we are all imposters, we don't have to do things the way we've been told they've always been done.

This book is roughly chronological. It begins with an essay on failing gloriously that uses a framework that can be operationalized in ways that are safe (whether or not you work in academia). The next section, "Unlearning," takes you from my adjunct/sessional and substitute teacher days to my online teaching days (2003 – 2009), and it picks apart the ways I had to unlearn what teaching could be. The next section recounts events that are largely contemporaneous with the first, but focuses instead on the social context of my work. The final two sections of the book take place largely in that period in which I started on the tenure track as a digital humanities person (2010 to about 2014). I did not know what 'digital humanities' meant, either for my teaching or for my research. The book concludes with some reflections on what digital humanities might be, and what a digital archaeology could be, building on work I've done since 2014. If there are tensions and contradictions it is because nothing is smooth or straightforward; my thinking and my teaching have evolved. There is value in taking a microscope to things we once wrote, we once said, we once thought.

I share these stories with you because, when I see them collected here, I see a thread that I couldn't see nearly twenty years ago when I started. My hope is that it helps the other imposters out there in navigating their own personal mazes, to wherever they lead, academia or elsewhere. I'm imagining you to be somewhere on your grad school journey, possibly at that same point I was when I stepped into the air. I write for the imposter I was and the imposter I continue to be. I write in the hopes that there's something here in these stories that will give you the support you need at the moment you need it. These are *stories*. They are not academic articles. They sometimes have footnotes and references, but sparingly. Citation is a gift, an act of accomplice-ship (Weiss); there is a choice to be made when we cite, in whose work we lift up, whose work becomes the foundation for our own. We become accomplices. Perhaps these choices I've made will confirm for you that I am, indeed, an imposter.

We're all imposters, but that's because we're always learning. The day I think I know what I'm doing will be the day to move on.

This volume has benefited enormously from the generous reading of the anonymous peer reviewers who engaged with a much more disjointed version. I am grateful for their suggestions and engagement, and apologize for making the experience harder than it ought to have been. Bill Caraher saw the potential, encouraged me throughout, and made the process intellectually rewarding. Sara Perry has exemplified the "generous thinking" that Kathleen Fitzpatrick argues for in her recent volume on how the university can be less confrontational and more collaborative. Luck and serendipity and generous thinking: If Lea Stirling hadn't advertised for a post-doc, if Lea hadn't been the kind of person who could say, "We didn't quite get what you were on about in your application, but it sounded interesting . . . so let's find out!" If John Bonnett and Kevin Kee hadn't been intrigued by the idea of agent-based modeling. If Alan Liu hadn't said, "Why aren't you blogging this?" If Lisa St. Louis hadn't posted the job advertisement for the liberal arts college. Colleen Morgan, Quinn Dombrowski, Bethany Nowviskie, Kisha Supernant, Katherine Cook, Donna Yates, Morag Kersel, Steph Halmhofer, Sharon Leon, Kathleen Fitzpatrick, Lee Skallerup, Lynne Goldstein, Lorna Richardson, Neha Gupta, Beth Compton, Jolene Smith, Sarah Bond, Dominique Marshall, Danielle Kinsey, Jenn Evans, Pat Moore, Eric Kansa, Ethan Watrall, Cristina Wood, Kaitlin Wainwright, Elise Bigley, Rob Blades, Hollis Peirce, Tamara, Carys, and Conall, my students and so many others—you know who you are—to all of you who've shared your own fails, whose example and scholarship I admire, and to all of you who have taken a chance on me, who have been generous, who have *put up with me*: thank you.

Failing Gloriously

What follows is a slightly edited version of the talk I gave at the Institute on Digital Archaeology Method & Practice at Michigan State University in the summer of 2015. Led by Lynne Goldstein and Ethan Watrall (and discussed by Watrall in "Building Scholars and Communities of Practice in Digital Heritage and Archaeology" in Advances in Archaeological Practice 7.2 https://doi.org/10.1017/aap.2019.1) the Institute was a two-week experience over two years that brought together private, public, established, and emerging scholars to learn together what digital archaeology could be. My role was to talk about failure, especially, but not necessarily, of things digital. The talk was my first real attempt at making sense of what had been still rather nebulous: what do you think you know about failing in public? It had only been a few years since my first formal I'm-an-academic-now project, The HeritageCrowd Project, had collapsed; the post-mortem for that project can be found in Part Three.

"You know nothing, Jon Snow!"

Jon Snow, of Game of Thrones/Westeros fame, is not a tactical genius, if the Battle of the Bastards was any indication. Yet he is fortunate in that he has some good advisors handy, like Ser Davos:

"You go on. You fight for as long as you can. You clean up as much of the shit as you can."
"I don't know how to do that. I thought I did, but I failed."
"Good. Now go fail again."

(season six, episode 3)

I like this little exchange, because what Ser Davos is arguing for is the productive fail. Unfortunately, Jon Snow rarely seems to learn the hard lessons. If you don't learn from the fail, then, well, "you know nothing."

I have no really good memory of where I first heard of the idea of the productive fail. I was a classicist once: the idea is at least as old as Greco-Roman antiquity. Propertius: Quod si deficiant vires, audacia certe laus erit: in magnis et voluisse sat est. Alcman: πῆρά τοι μαθήσιος ἀρχά. That is to say, "So what if you fail? Boldness itself will be enough to win praise: in great endeavors it is enough to have tried," and "Trying is the first step of learning." You get the idea. For as long as we've been human, there's always been someone saying, "Walk it off!" As Chumbawumba once sang, "I get knocked down, but I get up again, you're never going to keep me down!"

It's not a new idea, and it's not a profoundly deep idea, but it is a political idea, and it's a dangerous idea. It is dangerous in that without a strategy for dealing with the things that break, a strategy for failing productively, a fail is indeed a disaster and causes harm. For instance, the modern university puts all of the risks of innovative teaching on the instructor, with few supports in place. "Move fast and break things," Facebook's early mantra, has caused untold damage to civil society. It is political in that who gets to fail and suffer the consequences (or not) is a function of identity and power.

I'm a middle-aged white guy on the internet. When I first started blogging about my work in 2006, I did not realize the degree to which I was protected by that identity, by the privilege I had. Work by scholars like Katherine Cook makes it clear:

> Digital technologies (especially the Web) were sold to us as democratizing tools that would transform the inequities inherent in communications, research, and

institutional structures. When the shortcomings started to become visible, risk and danger were marketed to us as part of what everyone goes through to create good research and art, to innovate, to be successful. But that was not true either: some people are forced to take on more risk than others. The lines of privilege and power are far more insidious in our technology-drenched worlds than those who benefit from it care to recognize, let alone address. (Cook 398)

Having a strategy to deal with things that break or do not work or go wrong is not the same thing as valorizing risk or promoting failure for failure's sake. I'm not saying that I have the answer. But I think I can at least gesture toward an approach that begins to move the needle.

To fail productively, one has to be aware of the multiple contexts of that fail to find the valuable experience. To fail gloriously is to use the privileges that you have, as you are able, to make it safe for others to fail.

If you're not building other people up, why are you even here? A glorious fail is first and foremost an act of generosity. I recognize in this idea that I am allied with what Kathleen Fitzpatrick has called "generous thinking," that is, "a mode of engagement that emphasizes listening over speaking, community over individualism, collaboration over competition, and lingering with the ideas that are in front of us rather than continually pressing forward to where we want to go" (Fitzpatrick 4).

But competition is everything in academia, and so academia is not set up to recognize productive failure. Indeed, in a competitive system, failure necessarily has to be punished. The systems and meshworks, the entangled flows of power and money and incentives that make up academia are fragile, and failure is seen as a rupture, a breaking, a threat. The ideology of "fail fast" that comes to us from the technosphere imagines a situation dealing with complex systems that can be perturbed to new, more productive and efficient configurations, as if this is a moral or ethical goal.

In academia, this has the effect of corrupting research. Everything is always presented as a win (we also know this as "p-hacking"). I went looking for "fail" in archaeological literature. I built a topic model with 100 topics of nearly 20,000 archaeology articles from across the English-speaking world, from the 1930s onward (you can explore it for yourself at graeworks.net/digitalarchae/20000/). Do we ever talk about research that doesn't confirm a hypothesis? Do we ever try to replicate someone else's study? I would have thought there'd be something, given the processual turn in archaeology and the new archaeology and scientific archaeology more generally. If this macroscopic perspective on the historiography of (English-speaking) archaeology is any indication, the answer is no. The incentives of professional practice mean that we don't want to hear about things that didn't work. We spin our words, we carefully prune to present work in the best light.

To fail productively would mean an honest assessment of what actually happened. To fail gloriously would be to change the system so that honesty would not be seen as a radical act.

If we knew where the dead ends were, the things that didn't work—if we were not hiding our fear of being found out—would we not produce better research? Better teaching? Healthier relationships? A stronger academy?

My name is Shawn Graham, and I am an imposter in this world. I have screwed up so many times. So many times have I tried to put the best possible gloss on things, only to see the work immediately vanish in obscurity. It feels like I didn't begin to gain any kind of traction until I started giving it all away, the things that worked, the things that didn't, on my blog. When I became an official academic again (after eight years of under-employment), it was against that context of trying to be open about what I was doing versus the show-no-weakness ethos of academia. It didn't help that I was also in a History department, with its own traditions and disciplinary expectations of what history was supposed to be. Even though the job ad said digital humanities, and even though everyone I spoke to expected me to define for them what digital humanities/digital history could be, my imposter syndrome was in high gear. I was the expert! God help us all.

Let's take a whistle-stop tour of some of my fails, at which point we'll try to retrieve something of value from them.

Fail number one: As a graduate student, I worked on the Tiber Valley Project at the British School at Rome. Part of this involved entering data from paper recording sheets into a custom-made Microsoft Access database. After several months of doing this, I still had a stack of sheets that I could not enter into the database because they had a particular ware that was not in the drop-down menus for the pottery forms. I had myself a little dig inside the database and figured out how I could add the ware to the options. Presto, my backlog was cleared! Of course, not really understanding the implications of what I'd done, I managed to break so much of the underlying dependencies and reports that I set that aspect of the project back months starting from the moment I "fixed" things to the moment my fix was discovered. (I'm sorry, Helen.)

Fail number two: As a new member of the History department, I was interested in how Wikipedia generated knowledge, and so I assigned my students a task. Let's collaboratively update a Wikipedia page on the history of our region and see what happens next. The idea was to give the students first-hand experience of collaborative knowledge building and peer review. I also wanted the students to engage with ideas concerning whose voice got heard on Wikipedia. These were first-year students who had arrived at university with very clear ideas of what proper historians did—and Wikipedia (after years of injunctions against it) was not proper history. I had built up to the day with a series of scaffolded exercises that I thought would mitigate this, but I was wrong. All of my actual history majors were "sick" that day, despite my scaffolding, and did not participate.

Another example, fail number three: do you remember the game company, Infocom? They had a magazine advertisement that sticks with me. It showed a brain with its parts lit up in different colors. The headline was something like, "The Most Powerful Graphics Engine in the World." By the early 90s, Infocom was fighting a rear-guard action against the emergence of graphics-based games. But I remembered how immersive, how powerful, those text-based games had been, so I wrote one for my students in a class about the Roman city and countryside. We had been studying various maps and other top-down representations of that space. With the text-based game, that top-down representation couldn't be relied on. Instead, they would have to read and imagine the landscape from their character's position on the ground. The idea was to represent a Roman conception of space as a sequence of what comes next as well as to give the students a taste of way-finding in the Roman world through social interactions. Play a game versus read a paper—it should have been a no-brainer, I thought. And yet, the entire class balked. Flat out refused to play.

On a similar note, I remember the very first grad seminar I taught: fail number four. I had never experienced a North American graduate program, and by the time the students got to my course, most of them had been well-disciplined in what to expect from graduate seminars in history. I framed the course as an experiment in digital history: "How can we use augmented reality to tell history?" This was in 2011, and the technologies involved were not in any sense easy to use. But I felt we had a good vibe going in the class. Work was being produced. Interesting work! Powerful work! And yet, I received the worst teaching evaluation scores in the entire department, making for a rather inauspicious beginning for the untenured assistant professor. On those evaluations, which were filled out at perhaps the lowest time of the year, most comments were a variation on "If the tech doesn't work, will I fail?" and "How is this history?" and "I know how to write essays, I don't know what an A looks like here so I don't know what to do." Other comments suggested the idea of "experimenting" was an unfair thing to do with students about to hit the job market.

We all have fails like this, lurking in our closet. The question is, how do we make these productive? How do we make these glorious? The benefit of having a system for classifying our fails is that it can highlight elements in common between disparate episodes. Once classified, we can figure out what to do about them. Once classified, we have a language for talking about them that removes the personal oh-no-I-screwed-up and gives us a bit of critical distance. This distance can also serve to give us a degree of protection.

Brian Croxall and Quinn Warnick have an outstanding essay on failure and its role in teaching in Digital Pedagogy in the Humanities, which I find enormously useful. For Croxall and Warnick, there are four kinds of fails:

1. Technological Failure
2. Human Failure
3. Failure as Artifact
4. Failure as Epistemology

My examples above might be classified like this:

- The Tiber Valley Project Database: Type 2, in that I did not know what I did not know. At the time, I

thought I was dealing with a technological failure, but I was flat out wrong about that.
- The Wikipedia assignment: Type 2—the scaffolding focused on the wrong aspects of the work and did not address the powerful stories about what constitutes "proper" venues for work.
- Augmented reality for environmental history and the interactive fiction: Type 1 and Type 2—the technology did not work as advertised (and the API for one of the AR platforms we used changed in the middle of our experiment); the game of being a student was not confronted/disrupted sufficiently. That is to say: students are well trained in how to fulfill the "compulsory figures" of academia, as Daniel Paul O'Donnell (2012) puts it (the essays and midterms). I did not make it safe for the students to do this new thing I wanted.

Croxall and Warnick's taxonomy was something of a revelation for me. It crystallized things that I had been blundering towards. Quinn Dombrowski has an even more complete taxonomy of fail, drawing on her experiences with for instance DiRT, and Project Bamboo. Had I these taxonomies earlier when I was having those experiences in the first place, I might have retrieved something of value for the students (and myself). As the simpler of the two, let's begin with Croxall and Warnick's.

Their schema for classifying and understanding the types of fail we encounter also implies a strategy at the outset for dealing with the inevitable human or technological failures. Type 3—failure as artifact—means to accept that the fail is going to happen and to build into the course or research the examination of the fail itself as an object of study. Fail becomes a pedagogy, a way of being, when we hit Type 4 and conceive of failure as epistemology, for it gives us license to actively seek out ways of breaking the technologies in the first place. We change our focus from product to process, and we craft teaching, learning, and research activities accordingly.

As we engage with digital technologies, whether for research or public history/archaeology, we need to teach students how to create, how to craft, the compelling stories that the technology permits us to see. No one knows how to do this innately. It is not obvious, and it carries real risks. In order to move to a glorious failure though, we have to do one final thing and share it: failure as open reflection. It is in this last step that we expand our productive engagement from the confines of our own teaching or research into the wider world and make it safe for those without power or position, or who are in precarious employment, to fail too.

My very public fail, the loss of the HeritageCrowd website (which I discuss later in this volume in "How I Lost the Crowd"), was an accidental glorious failure brought about by despair. As a new hire, the university gave me a small sum of money to start my research program. Trying to fit into what I thought of as the department's vision for my role (as a contributor to the public history program), I came up with a project that would use the Ushahidi platform (developed to allow real-time mapping of a crisis) to solicit and then to map places of intangible cultural heritage. Because I—quite frankly—did not know what I was doing, I left the site I made using that platform open to automated attacks. There was the human failure (Type 2) in that I didn't understand enough about the open source community to know to pay attention to the forum and discussions—especially the security discussions. That left my code open to attack (Type 1).

When the site collapsed (it went offline, and its database was corrupted with Viagra advertisements that would be used, as I understand it, to seed spam), I wrote a post-mortem about what had happened and posted it online. In my despair—my imposter status having been publicly confirmed—I inadvertently moved to a Type 3 fail, where I discussed and studied what went wrong. That single blog post may have been the most important post I ever made, for it led directly to the change in perspective that I needed in order to teach and learn this bundle of things that is digital humanities—a Type 4 fail. Sharing it online used the privilege I had to help develop a genre of discussing fails in a productive way.

Mine certainly wasn't the first public discussion of a project that did not come together in the way its creators wanted, but the experience became formative for everything I've done since. I had never been trained to discuss or acknowledge the things that did not work. Framing what happened the way I did was liberating, for I realized the success or failure of the project was independent of my identity. Rather, it is epistemology, it is artifact, and following Croxall and Warwick, it is pedagogy. My job, I discovered, is to make it safe to try things out by emphasizing this framework for process rather than product.

But consider:

> When we risk going too far, we discover how far we can go. In today's era of motivational speak, risk has been singularly rebranded as a badge of honour. In turn, risk is considered a cornerstone of art, innovation, creativity, and ultimately, change. Perhaps ironically, then, it is the #MeToo, Idle No More, and Black Lives Matter movements, among others, that have shone a light on the dark underbelly of taking chances: the demand for individuals to step forward and share their voice paints targets on the already vulnerable and marginalized for fear- and anger-filled hate and aggression, repeatedly

and relentlessly beating down the voices of change. Often forced to choose between the long-term, abstract risk of doing nothing (and, therefore, nothing ever changing for the better) and the immediate and often personal risk of trying to confront the system, the individuals leading the charge of these movements, in the name of equity, security, and inclusivity, face harassment, abuse, suspicion, imprisonment, and violence. (Cook 409)

Personal security has to come first. One way I suggest for shifting some of the risks to personal security is to frame the work within this discussion of the kind of fail with which we're dealing. The second part is to move the discussion toward fail as something we study (rather than something inherent to us), and then to a process, to a way we iterate through what we study.

While Croxall and Warnick's taxonomy functions as a tool toward better pedagogy, Dombrowski's taxonomy reminds us of the human costs and dangers, because it is generated from the experience of the very real risks she underwent working on, and shutting down, projects including the DiRT directory of digital research tools. She frames the different fails by their consequences, learning value, and sharing value. She sees, for people working in the digital humanities, that there are:

- Tech fails
- Career planning fails
- Communication fails
- Strategic fails
- Arbitrary (job market) fails
- Failures to probe assumptions
- Failures to acknowledge change
- Failures to forge a shared vision

- Failures to do right by others

It must be the archaeologist in me that wants to group and file Dombrowski's taxonomy into the simpler categories of Croxall and Warnick. That isn't necessary, however, because they are doing slightly different work here. In what follows, I will use Croxall and Warnick's schema in some of the reflections in Part One, "Unlearning." Part Two, "Getting Over Myself," can be viewed better through Dombrowski's categories, and those themes will be apparent. Part Three, "Fits and Starts and Fumbles," will draw from Croxall and Warnick, but shift thematically to Dombrowski's "Failure to do right by others." Indeed, I see failing gloriously, if it is to have any utility as a concept, as a fusion of doing right by others while trying to pick apart the interplay between digital tech and humans.

Part One

Unlearning

The first teaching gig I ever had was in 2002 for a continuing education class night course at the University of Reading. I was full of rigid terror, with no teacher training, knowing only that I had to teach them about "The Etruscans." Lectures. Quizzes. Essays. The full apparatus brought to bear on my students, who were all senior citizens and there for a bit of companionship, a bit of interest, on a Wednesday night.

As you can imagine, it didn't go very well. A little bit of humanity/humility, some confidence in letting go, a little less being-a-twerp, would have made an enormous difference. The pieces in this section are about some of the hardest lessons I ever had to learn, about the things that really matter, when all is said and done. Be human. Don't be a jerk. Be kind. The stories told in this section are all about failures at the intersection of our training, our expectations, and our systems.

"The First Time" is a reflective diary I kept on my first teaching experience with undergraduate students, a few months after my unfortunate Etruscans. For my purposes here, I have annotated it where I cringe to read it now. There is a tension between unrealistic expectations and the scaffolding—or not—that I provided. There are human fails throughout that first experience. Many are mine, but some are systemic issues beyond the power of a contingent academic to address. But what strikes me most, now, is my lack of empathy, and my floundering to get the ideas across.

In "On Teaching High School" I draw direct lessons from the hardest teaching experience I had, working with boys in a vocational class at a high school in Western Quebec in 2004/5. If you *really* want to learn how to teach, spend some time in a high school. The next piece, "The Smoking Crater" (2007), explores some Type 1 and Type 2 fails and their impacts on the institution and its students. In "Papers, Please" (2009), the Kafkaesque systems that surround for-profit education are driven home by my trying to cross the US–Canada border, and they provide fodder for reflection on what this does to our teaching. For once, my imposter syndrome was actual rather than metaphorical.

The First Time

My graduate training did not involve any teacher training. It involved no professionalization. It was purely research. Eight months after graduation, I saw a job advertisement for a visiting lectureship in Roman Archaeology. I did not realize that "visiting" was code for precarious, adjunct teaching. I applied, got the job, and started wondering *now what*. I was hired one week prior to the start of term to teach a class designed by somebody else. This person had included an oral examination for the final assessment exercise. I had never conducted an oral examination before or prepped anyone to take one. Hell, I'd only had my own viva (thesis defense) a few months previously. This was about to be my first experience with teaching a "regular" undergraduate class (as I imagined undergraduates: full-time students, 18–21 years old). I signed up for the university's post-graduate certificate in learning & teaching in higher education, in the hopes that I would learn enough to be able to do the oral examination by the end of the term, enough to teach properly.

As part of the course work for the certificate, I had to keep a reflective diary on my teaching and submit it at the end of the program. As I reread the diary below, I cringe at my errors and my assumptions about my students. I cringe at the style I'm writing with too. It is in many ways inauthentic (I'm clearly writing for an audience of one: the program convener), and it misses the point of what a reflective diary could be: an opportunity for growth.

There's something to be said for keeping a diary of your teaching. But it's a helluva thing to read it over again years later.

October 14, 2003

Do my students understand what they are doing in my class? Do they see the point of what we are trying to accomplish?

[*Well done pastShawn, putting it all on the students, slow slow clap.*]

Last week's class felt like an overall flop—stony, unresponsive faces, no flicker of life anywhere. Part of the problem I think is that I tried to fit too much into one class... In today's class, there was much more dialogue, with a backwards and forwards discussion of the ideas, with students bringing some of their own experiences to bear. One or two have some formal archaeological experience, which helps, and others have traveled. The Romans are not "just like us," so experience of foreign cities/cultures helps get people into the right mindset. One student, E, informed me that she has no idea what I am alluding to half the time, which I should have found out on day one. On the plus side, she is one of those students who has no fear of saying "I don't know" or "I don't get it," which I think the rest of the class is secretly pleased about, because it forces me to slow down and rethink what I'm trying to say. When she says "Whoa!" I have to concentrate on "connecting-the-dots," which is a difficulty I've always had in my academic work. I tend to assume that everybody else sees the same connections that I do.

[*This continues to be an issue for me, as you no doubt can tell. Cherish the students who are bold enough to say woah!*]

October 20, 2003

I wanted to find out if the students were with me, following on from last week's reflection. (During the first few meetings my main concern was simply to get the class rolling. I think I was in panic mode, more worried about what I knew than on what my students were there for.) We talked about how the seminar presentations will be graded. I want them to mark each other's seminar presentations, using the same criteria as I use, so that when it comes time for the oral exam, they will have a good understanding of what constitutes an excellent presentation, and what the examiners are looking for. In that spirit, I asked them to mark my performance so far in the class (anonymously).

[*This is a bit better pastShawn: trust your students and give them meaningful ways to direct the progress of the class. Let go.*]

I found out some hard truths. They liked the interaction between myself and them, the back-and-forth, but thought that everything went on for far too long. They also found my lectures hard to follow, and would like more illustrative material. What I found very interesting was that they wanted more of the "nuts-and-bolts" of classical archaeology: architectural orders, building types, narrative history, etc. So much for my anthropological slant on the growth of cities!

[*Did you ask yourself why that was?*]

October 27, 2003

Today was the first of the seminar presentations. I have designed the seminars to act as preparation for the oral examination. This university has a defined set of criteria for oral presentation assessments. What I wanted to do was to use self and peer assessment to guide the students toward what an acceptable presentation during the exam would be like. I prepared a handout two weeks ago called "Points to Ponder." I directed the students to remember the learning outcomes for this class, and to structure their presentations around those outcomes. I also asked the students to write and hand in a brief synopsis of what they intended to accomplish during the seminar; after the seminar, they were to write a synopsis of what they did accomplish, and to indicate where they felt they could have made improvements. For students listening and participating in the discussion, I prepared an anonymous marking sheet to hand in afterward. My idea was that these marking sheets would help the other students stay engaged, and would help them become familiar with what I, as the tutor, was looking for in a presentation. The following week I intended to discuss with the student how the seminar went, how the other students felt it went, and areas for improvement for the oral examination.

[*This is not bad, pastShawn. A bit stick-in-the-mud, and verging on busywork at times, but it's apparent some of what you were learning in the training course you were trying to incorporate. I see your effort to build a community invested in each other's success here.*]

Three students presented. It soon became obvious that although the stronger students had understood what I intended for the presentations, the weaker student did not. Her information was solid, but her presentation did not convey the information to the rest of the class particularly well. Her presentation did, however, stimulate discussion in a way the stronger presentations did not. This, I think, is partly explained by the class dynamic. The weaker student is usually very garrulous, and her sudden shyness elicited a sympathetic response from the class. The other two students were so confident in their material that discussion was limited to technical points. I need to spend some more time on the basics of presentations and public speaking. I did not penalize her as harshly as I might have, realizing that to a degree I did not adequately prepare her and that public speaking for the shy can be torture.

[*What are you trying to accomplish pastShawn? What did you actually want the students to learn in your class? You're teaching to the exam! What is the pedagogical point of a viva voce examination? You never asked. You put this student through an excruciating ordeal. You jerk. You should have stood your ground. There was no real reason why you had to do the viva voce style. Know the rules! Also, you're writing like a pompous twit. Stop it.*]

November 24, 2003

While some of the presentations have been very good indeed, others have been simply deplorable. I have made myself available after class, by appointment, and set up a dedicated email address for them to reach me, and no one has contacted me or come to me for extra help or guidance. This shows in the quality of their presentations. They cite their sources but rarely, and when they do, the source is not tremendously reliable. Most of the poor presentations have relied on the internet exclusively, and I get the impression that they were cobbled together immediately prior to class.

[*AND WHO'S FAULT IS THAT? And there's a bit of irony, you complaining about students using the internet . . .*]

Last week was our museum trip to the London Museum, to see its display on Roman Londinium. This was during the reading week, but I understood that many classes conducted field trips during this week. We had spent quite some time the week before arranging a day and time to meet that was convenient for everyone. On the agreed day, it rained quite hard. Although the museum is only thirty to forty-five minutes from the university, only one student showed up. This was extremely disappointing, to say the least. After a forty-minute wait, another student arrived. I had intended the visit to be fairly unstructured and allow students to follow their own interests, and I would act as an extra resource for them during the visit. I had also envisioned a treasure hunt, with the students divided into two teams, searching for displays and artifacts which tied into the learning outcomes.

[*Treasure hunts are fine, but . . . lacking in a bit of imagination? How many times have these students done that exact thing, at this exact museum? Oh pastShawn. But it was a disappointment, all the same. Perhaps something a bit less twee would have had a different result?*]

Today therefore I expressed my unhappiness with these recent developments. It is all well and good to try to structure my teaching around the needs and foci of the students, but if they do not participate . . . Which leads to the question, did they not come because they are not engaging with the class? Or did they not come because they are simply lazy? When I put the question to them directly, there was an embarrassed silence, and no response. Interestingly, each of them approached me individually afterwards with an excuse. Given that we had agreed on a day and time and place, and that they all had ample opportunity to warn me ahead of time that they couldn't make it for whatever reason, I'm inclined to think that our field trip fell victim to laziness. I really don't know what else I can do to engage these students.

[Oh pastShawn. Lazy? Could you have tried to understand the context that your students were operating in? You assumed the students were just like you. Your teaching was always about you, about your terror, about your state of mind, about your situation. You never met your students halfway. If the students have been to the museum before—and treasure hunt— why should they bother? What would they have got out of it? In the calculus of students' time, it wasn't a trip with much value. The outcome is perfectly rational.]

December 15, 2003

When I started this course, I relied quite heavily on my lecture notes and worked from the idea that "lecturers lecture." This was not a particularly good strategy for a number of reasons. Formal lectures are a cost-effective way of delivering a large amount of information to a large number of people, but not necessarily for those people to retain that information. For the number of students in the Roman Cities class, it was in fact faintly ridiculous to be lecturing to them from a prepared text. Asking "Any questions?" at the end did not achieve anything but a quiet stare. I soon changed my style, abandoning formal lectures and lecture notes. I started to extemporize, actually talking with the students about the topic, rather than speaking *at* them. This frequently touched off fierce discussion amongst the students themselves, with me needing only to speak now and again to guide the discussion around the learning outcomes. My handouts became clearer and more structured as I began to rely on them to structure my lectures, rather than using pre-written lectures.

[*Thank bloody goodness pastShawn. I was beginning to lose hope.*]

Looking back at the material that I have given to them, I think that the biggest mistake that I made was at the outset with the course handout. I did not divide up the bibliography into logical coherent sections, leaving them to decide which articles/books to read and to guess which would probably be relevant to the scheduled topic. If I were to do this again, I would be more careful about clearly indicating what should be read when, what was absolutely crucial, and so on. I did in fact provide the students each week with photocopies of crucial articles and book excerpts (to forestall the inevitable "I tried the library, but the book/journal wasn't there" whine) once I realized the mistake.

[*It's astonishing, but I had to learn this: it is not self-evident why a particular reading is assigned. It's not cheating to give hints as to what you're hoping the students might start to understand as they read.*]

As for the seminars, after my quiet discussion with them about their responsibilities as students (and the fact that their success on the oral exam and the final exam depended to a certain extent on everybody doing their part in the presentations), the quality picked up again, and there was a marked improvement in attendance. I think perhaps that when they thought I wouldn't care about them attending, or doing well, they themselves cared little; when it became obvious that I was extremely disappointed in them, it helped rekindle their own commitment to the class.

[*Puts hands over eyes, shakes head, walks away. Clearly, there was a reason I wasn't getting hired to permanent gigs.*]

On Teaching High School

"Hey! Hey Sir!"

Some words just reach out and grab your attention. "Sir" is not normally one of them, but I was at the Shawville Fair, and that term isn't often used in the midway. I turned, and saw before me a student from ten years previously. We chatted; he was married, had a step-daughter, another daughter on the way. He'd apprenticed, become a mechanic. He was doing well. I was glad to see him.

"So, you still teaching us assholes up at the school?"

No, I was at the university now. "You guys weren't assholes."

A Look. "Yes, we were. But there were good times, too, eh?"

Ten years earlier, I held my first full-time, regular teaching contract at the local high school. The year before that, I was a regular-rotation substitute teacher. Normally one would need a teaching certificate to teach at a high school, but strangely enough newly minted teachers never seem to consider rural or more remote schools. Everyone wants to teach in the city. Having at least stood in front of students in the past, I was about the best short-term solution around. Toward the latter part of that year holes had opened up in the schedule, and I was teaching every day. This transmuted into a regular gig teaching Grade 9 computing, Grade 9 geography (a provincially mandated course), and Grade 10/11 technical drawing.

And Math for Welders.

The school is formally a "polyvalente," meaning a school where one could learn trades. However, our society's bias against trades, and years of cuts to the English system in Quebec (and asinine language laws which, amongst other things, mandate that only books published in Quebec can be used as textbooks) meant that all of the trade programs were dead. In the last decade, this last-gasp program had been established in the teeth of opposition (which meant these students were watched very carefully indeed—and they knew it). Instead of taking high math and other courses targeted at the university bound, these students could take welding math. They also worked in a metal shop. If they could pass my course and pass the exam for their 'welding ticket', they could graduate high school and begin apprenticeships directly.

The welding program was conceived as a solution for students (typically boys, though there were a few girls in the program over the years) who had otherwise fallen through the cracks in the system. It was intense. These students had never had academic success. They were older than their peers, having fallen behind. They had all manner of social issues, family issues, learning difficulties, you name it.

And they were all mine. Not only did I teach technical drawing and math (so right there, two or three hours of face-to-face time per day, every day), I was also their homeroom teacher. At our school, homeroom was not just about morning attendance; it was also a kind of inter-grade study hall. Other classes had a mix of grades in these homerooms, meaning older students could work with younger on homework, personal stuff, whatever; but my homeroom had no admixture. It was just me and the welders.

I learned a lot about teaching over those years.

I could tell you a lot of stories about pain and stress. I've never been quite so near to quitting, to tears, to breaking down, to screaming at the world. I completed a PhD! I was from the same town! I'd beaten the system! Did that not earn me some respect? Was I not owed?

No.

And that was the hardest lesson right there. In fact, although I thought myself humble when I started the job (after two years of slogging in the adjunct/sessional world, hustling for contract heritage work, and so on), I still had a hard time disentangling my expectations of what students should be from my notion of the kind of student I was. Those first two months, up to Thanksgiving, might've been a lot easier if I had.

I also underestimated how hard it would be to earn respect. I figured a PhD meant I'd already earned it, in the eyes of the world. But I hadn't counted on how prevalent the "If you were any good you wouldn't be working here" attitude was.

Once, one of the students fell asleep in class. What do you do, as a novice teacher? You wake him up. You take him into the hallway to 'deal' with him. And then I sent him up to the office. What I didn't know was what was going on at home, outside of school: his dad was long gone, and suffice to say, he was looking after his siblings and trying to keep the house running on his own. He was having to stay up at night to keep everyone else safe.

And god help me, I was giving him shit for not drawing his perspective drawings correctly, for falling asleep.

With time, I began to earn their respect. It helped that at school functions I had no fear of standing up and making a fool of myself by doing whatever silly activity the pep leaders had devised. "He's a goof but he's OUR goof!" seemed to be the sense. I learned that I had to stop being a teacher and start being my students' advocate. Who else was going to stand up for them? Everyone else had already written them off.

In some corners of the school, there was a firmly held conviction that these students were getting off easy, that somehow what they were doing was less intellectually challenging. There were some ugly staffroom showdowns. Welding math involves a lot of geometry, trigonometry, finances, and mental calculation. It's not easy in any way, shape, or form.

Tradespeople in Canada frequently work in Imperial units, while officialdom works in metric. Calculating, switching, tallying, laying out complex three dimensional shapes onto flat sheet metal: these are all non-trivial things! "Sir, that's the first time I passed a math test since Grade 4!" said one student around about October.

The first test since Grade 4. My god, what have we done to ourselves, to create a system that sets students up for failure? And none of these students were dumb, in the sense that students use. When I lost most of the class to moose hunting season, I had them explain to me exactly what they did once they got back. There erupted an extremely complicated discussion of fish and game laws and licensing, camouflage and the behavior of game, cleaning and preparing the meat.... These were smart people. They never hesitated to call me out when what I was saying to them was nonsense or not making sense.

"Sir," a voice in the back would say, "what the fuck are you talking about?" You can't get angry about language. This is how they've learned to speak. But imagine: a student in your class actually taking the time to explain that they don't understand, and to show you where they lost you? These students did that! Once I learned to take the time to listen, it turned out that they had a lot to say.

It was never easy, working with this class. At the end of the year, I was completely drained. A tenured teacher came back from sick leave, and I was bumped from my position. Unemployed again. Look at that from my students' perspective: "Here's a guy, finished first in high school, got a PhD. Came back home without a job. Ends up working with us and then loses his job again afterward. Maybe, just maybe, doing the whole academic thing they push isn't the thing. Maybe working with my hands, welding, machining—I'll always have work. If I can figure out how to plan the best cuts in this sheet of metal so that I don't waste any money. If I can pass the welding exam. If I don't get my girlfriend pregnant. If I pass on the blow this weekend and go to work."

Did some of them think that? I'd like to think so. We bickered, we locked horns, but once I proved to them that I was on their side, I'd like to think the good stuff outweighed the bad. I certainly know that it did wonders for me as a teacher. First and foremost, it forced me to get over myself. I learned that:

- Nobody owes me anything;
- What I was like as a student is no guide to what my students are like as students;
- I need to ask "How do I make it safe to try something, How do I make it safe for students to admit that I'm making not an ounce of sense to them?"
- I need to not assume I know anything about my students' backgrounds;
- I need to make my expectations crystal clear for what constitutes proof-of-learning;
- I need to be part of the life of my school/community so that my students see that I'm invested in them.

Later, I won a postdoc position at the University of Manitoba and began teaching in distance and online education. That helped me transmogrify into whatever this digital humanities/digital archaeology thing is. That's the final lesson right there. I have a PhD in the finer points of the Tiber Valley brick industry. Don't be afraid to change: your PhD is not you. It's just proof that you can see a project through to the end, that you are tenacious, and that you can put the pieces together to see something new. Without the PhD, I could never have worked with those students.

I was glad to see Jeremy at the fair that year.

The Smoking Crater

> Some humans would do anything to see if it was possible to do it. If you put a large switch in some cave somewhere, with a sign on it saying "End-of-the-World Switch. PLEASE DO NOT TOUCH," the paint wouldn't even have time to dry. (Terry Pratchett, *Thief of Time*)

In this story, I have returned to Western Quebec after twelve months of pretending to be an academic again (that stint as a postdoc at the University of Manitoba). That is to say, I had no job and would do damn near anything in order to eat. The advertisement was an invitation to join a new online liberal arts college in the US that would offer a two-year associate degree. The successful applicant would teach Roman history online and would help manage Moodle, the learning management system. I'd never used Moodle before, but I'd seen it in the one-click package installer on the control panel for the domain space I'd bought. I fired up the computer, opened the panel, and clicked the button. A couple of hours and a few tutorials later, I felt able to write the application letter. I'd used a learning management system as a postdoc, so I felt that I could learn whatever I needed to know fairly quickly. What could go wrong?

The college, it turned out, was a three-person band of merry subversives. It was funded by a society who were certain that a return to the Classics would restore American morals and decency. Fortunately, they never really looked closely at the curriculum we developed. Being inclined to tinker around the innards of things, I soon found myself entirely in charge of managing the Moodle system. We experimented with all sorts of things; anything we could think of to fold into Moodle, we did. I built an archaeological excavation inside of Second Life and tied the virtual artifacts to objects published at OpenContext.org. (Sorry, Eric). We used wikis and blogs (at the time, still quite novel). We examined and played video games featuring the ancient world.

And then one day came The Request.

"Can you upgrade Moodle to the latest version?"

I'd installed Moodle on my own server and it was easy. How hard could an upgrade be? So I pressed the upgrade button.

Imagine you're walking to your university. It's a pleasant enough day, the sun is warm, you're looking forward to class. You come around the corner, and there's nothing but a smoking crater where the university once stood.

This was the digital equivalent. And I was on dial-up internet.

I drove to the city, where the techiest friend I had lived. He was working nights at the time, but I pounded on his door.

"Please, you gotta help me. I've nuked the university."

It took ten hours of painstaking work to figure out what had gone wrong. It turned out that the original developer for the college had custom coded a front end for the college that would handle taking students' tuition money and enrolling them in various courses in Moodle. When I pressed the button to upgrade Moodle, all of these custom hooks into Moodle broke. We printed out every PHP file in the system and laid them on the floor. We traced the dependencies between files, literally drawing out the connections, on the floor. We walked through every call from start to finish, manually working out what was loading what and when. Another ten hours and we had the thing working again.

So before you press the button, ask yourself, are you ready to print out every file?

Returning to the fail typology, the issue here again was Type 1 and Type 2 fails intersecting in complex ways. The broader context of this non-profit institution was part of the culture wars that are such a feature of American higher education. The organization funding this college was definitely on the right-hand side of the spectrum. It recognized the potential power of controlling an educational institution, but at the same time took a curiously hands-off approach. The college was directed to target home-schooled high school students, providing them a sealed space for higher education that would not require them to move or encounter the world beyond their current bubble. Our merry band of subversives could teach Classics meant to complicate and unsettle the worldview that was funding the work. It's not that we were teaching Classics slanted to the opposite end of the political spectrum. The curriculum we taught would not have been out of place in a museum education program in the UK. It was more that by occupying the center we were already so far to the left. Perhaps it was a function of targeting that particular demographic that led to such a hands-off approach. But it also meant that appropriate levels of oversight and staffing to do the work were similarly skimped. Thus, the contractor who wired the payment system into the learning management system could do the job, but didn't need to leave any documentation.

But the greater failure was this: no one noticed the smoking crater.

This is a human failure on a monumental scale. You can print out every file, you can design every course and every pathway, you can build a wonderful system—but what does it say if an entire organization can disappear without comment? Even from its students?

Papers, Please

Western Quebec is one of the poorer regions of Quebec, especially its rural parts. Internet connectivity lags far, far behind. Yet, with a satellite dish, online education was a (just) feasible option for me. In 2009 I applied for, and got, a job with an online university in Arizona. It had been a small, private, Baptist college with a focus on Christian education when it went bankrupt in 2003. It was purchased by investors who took its nascent online program and began pouring resources into attracting students from around the US with the promise of upward mobility, low cost, and flexibility. By 2009, its campus had stabilized at around 1000 students as I recall; online, it had approximately ten times that number. I had followed one of my collaborators from the previous online college (the one I knocked offline by accident). The job involved training faculty to teach online, to investigate student and faculty complaints about actions in the online classrooms, and to teach one or two courses (World Literature, as it happened). The lawyers for the university determined that though I would be living in Canada, I would need the right paperwork. This is when I was, in fact, called an imposter by someone with the legal power to make it stick. I wrote this in the immediate aftermath.

It began, as these things do, with a trip to the border by car. In order for me to work remotely, I needed to obtain TN status on my passport. This is a NAFTA (the North America Free Trade Agreement, in place until 2018) designation for certain professions, university teaching amongst them, allowing the free movement of labor. The websites I was reading left the impression that this is no big deal as well as easily obtainable (and only obtainable) from a customs agent at a crossing point.

A two-hour drive to the border and a two-hour interview later, I found myself denied entry into the United States. The major issue was that the agent didn't believe me when I said that one, I was an academic (correcting the agent's pronunciation of University of Reading probably didn't help), and two, the work involved teaching.

"Try this again, and you'll be arrested for fraud and perjury."

I was married, with a new baby on the way, and this was my best chance at decent employment. The humiliation stung as I tried to explain to the Canadian customs agent why I was denied entry and had to reenter Canada.

The clock was ticking. I called the university, and their advice was that there was nothing wrong with my credentials, or the job description, and that I should try again.

After being explicitly told that trying again would lead to arrest.

I had done nothing wrong but try to apply for my NAFTA rights. I spent some time online, which was a mistake. Don't read the websites that tell you what to do: they're from lawyers trying to sell their services, and they'll make you sick with worry.

I know I was. I puked. My wife talked me down from the edge, and I resolved to try again. After all, I really need the job. Together we walked through everything that had happened. I had left in high spirits and had my materials together in an old manila folder. I'd been dressed in standard thirty-some-year-old Rural Canadian. We also figured that crossing at our closest crossing point was a mistake in that, while Canada hugs the American border, America does not always hug back. The American side near us is a pretty rural, economically depressed, and remote spot that likely doesn't see many people trying to get NAFTA visas for online education work. Know your audience.

This time, I got a new haircut. Put on a new suit and tie. Collected all of my documents into a crisp and sharp portfolio. I grabbed every document I could think of, including my house taxes—a random fellow on a forum suggested this would be helpful (and it turned out, it was). And while I was still nervous, we figured that crossing in Toronto (US Customs has an outpost at the airport for Canadians to pre-clear if traveling to the US) would increase my chances of success—after all, it's the busiest airport in Canada in the richest and largest city in Canada and where else would all the NAFTA visas be given out as a regular occurrence? I even had *just* enough airline reward points that I could pull this off without ruining my credit card. I called the university up and said I was going to fly down to visit in order to get this visa.

Wednesday:

6:00 a.m. Get up, get dressed, drive to airport.
11:00 a.m. Embark on first leg of air journey: feeder airport to Toronto.
12:00 noon. Arrive in TO. Next flight: 1:30 p.m.
12:10 p.m. Present myself to customs pre-screening.
12:15 p.m. Agent begins to look at my papers (hey! everything's going great! hands are shaking, but that's normal for me, sharp tie and suit means I'm A Serious Person).
12:30 p.m. Agent informs me that everything looks great, but he's going on break, so new guy will handle things.
12:40 p.m. New guy picks up my folder.
1:30 p.m. Flight takes off. Shawn sits in waiting room, staring at shoes. Tie is uncomfortable.
2:00 p.m. New guy beckons me over. "Everything looks fine, but my supervisor wants to see a copy of the contract. Our fax machine is broken, so I'll take you out to the Air Canada

desk, you can use theirs. Then get a new flight booked."

2:30 p.m. Queuing for Air Canada desk, now that I've found it.

2:50 p.m. Agent gives me their fax number. Phone call later, and the non-signed copy of the contract is faxed to me in the airport (the original having been returned to Human Resources)

2:56 p.m. Resume queuing.

3:20 p.m. Very nice agent explains that since I booked the flight as a reward flight, I have to phone Aeroplan, and points me to the pay phones.

3:23 p.m. Elevator music.

3:56 p.m. Elevator music.

4:10 p.m. Agent. After much "can you please hold" I'm told that there are no flights for me, and I'll have to rebook for the following week.

4:30 p.m. American customs says, gee that's too bad. Here are your papers back, we would've stamped your passport, but you're not traveling today.

4:35 p.m. Resume queuing at Air Canada.

4:40 p.m. Same nice agent. I ask for a ticket back home. She was an absolute star, one of the only bright points in an otherwise long long day. She is outraged at Aeroplan, and begins to work some magic. She finds me a new ticket, this time to Los Angeles (with connection to final destination). Flight leaves at 5:50 p.m.

5:20 p.m. She runs me back to customs, jumping the queue, and takes me back into secondary processing. I sit down. She goes and talks to the second customs agent who looked at my stuff—who's about to have a shift break. There's another fellow with him. New fellow looks upset at being harangued by the ticket agent, other agent doesn't seem upset. Ticket agent leaves, says she'll be waiting outside with my itinerary, once it gets printed.

5:25 p.m. I get called over. "Why did you give us all these photocopies? You're supposed to give me originals!" shouts the newest agent. Previous agent points out that he took the photocopies. I present the originals. "Why did you get denied entry five days ago?" I retell my tale. This agent is not impressed, but other agent intervenes. "This contract isn't signed! Why should I let you in, with an unsigned contract!" I point out that the signed version has already been sent to HR, and I wouldn't have even bothered coming to the airport if HR hadn't said, Ok, great see you soon.

"Why haven't you got an I-94?"

"I don't know. What's an I-94?"

"We can't process you, without an I-94. This is an I-94. Fill it out!"

"This is in Spanish."

... nobody likes a smart arse ...

Other agent intervenes, fills out form. Silence ensues, then I'm sent to the cash register to pay the fees. TN status is mine!

5:44 p.m. I leave customs, proceed to security. Shoes off, laptop out, change in the bin. Old lady in front of me. My nervousness, stress, tiredness, and hunger attract attention.

5:48 p.m. I clear security. Shoelaces untied, I race down the looonnnnng corridor to the gate.

5:51 p.m. Gate is shut. Plane is gone. Air Canada lady says, "We paged you. You should've been here." New ticket for tomorrow morning is issued. Please leave airport.

6:00 p.m. Canada Customs. "You don't have anything to declare? No duty free?" I patiently explain—again—that I've missed a flight, and NO, I certainly WOULD NOT be doing ANY BLEEDIN' SHOPPING.

One should always be polite for customs agents.

> **7:00 p.m.** Safely ensconced in an airport hotel, I try to drown out the noise of the party next door with my pillows, hoping to get on the flight in the morning.

Thursday:

> **6:00 a.m.** Leave hotel for airport.
> **6:30 a.m.** In the customs queue.
> **6:35 a.m.** Cleared the queue. Angels sing; balloons fall from ceiling; fireworks.
> **8:00 a.m.** On plane to LAX.

No idea what time it is when I get to LAX, but I have to get from terminal one to terminal seven. This involves crossing several lanes of traffic. I re-check in for the final leg of the flight—a stroke of luck! I can fly standby on the earlier flight. All I have to do is clear security. I go up to the security level.

There's one x-ray machine.

For the entire bloody terminal.

The queue stretches out of the terminal, across the bridge to the parking garage, into the bright LAX smog. I miss the earlier flight.

Around 9:00 a.m. local time, I have arrived. One last leg to the hotel: where do I pick up the shuttle? Instructions are sought, given, and I stand out on the median, watching the shuttle go by, on a different road entirely.

The following day, I perform the journey in reverse.

I'd better like this job.

With imposter syndrome, it is normally only our internal voice who calls us "imposter." In this case, my inability to convince the customs agent still causes echoes in my life, especially since when I travel to the United States, I have to recount what happened back then to the agent on duty: I am an entry in a database. I shudder to think what the experience might be like now, in 2019. Was it worth it?

Over the next ten months, from my home in West Quebec, I use satellite internet to connect and start my day at work. The time I log on is noted. The time it takes me to hit "reply" to an email is counted. The number of "touches" (that is, any contact) I have with faculty, with other staff, with various systems, are all counted. Classes run in seven week blocks throughout the year. Courses have been designed by subject matter experts and are deployed to match student demand. There can be tens of sections for a particular course (each section is capped at twenty students). There can be no deviation from the course shell and its assignments.

Every assignment is run through Turn-it-in. Every few weeks, waves of plagiarism alerts have to be investigated because the plagiarism detection keeps flagging work from previous sections as stolen work. Turn-it-in makes its money from the students' captive work. The vast majority are false positives, a result of the fact that so many students are writing the same five-hundred-word "essays" using the same three permitted resources. Students file complaints over instructors not responding fast enough or not responding from the "right" perspective. Instructors file plagiarism complaints.

Tickets are filed in our tracking system for course shells that don't work correctly, or that have deployed partially, or have simply crashed. Our team covers every time zone. We meet via teleconference every week. Tickets get assigned. Targets are met. Student numbers increase. Ten months in, we are at 50,000 students online. The pace has increased every week. The size of our team has not.

One new faculty member asks me, given how these online courses provide so much of the materials one would normally create for oneself when teaching, if there was any way for the instructor to be truly creative in her teaching. I answer with a response that could be approved by the main office. I write that I too initially chafed at this when I first started, and you would have found me firmly in the camp that having so many of the materials pre-made was restrictive. But after a while, I write, I came to realize that there was a great deal of stealthy freedom involved in this structure. If you think of these pre-made course shells as a kind of seminar course, one where some library god has already created the readings and assignments for you, then you can bring all of your energies, your creativity, to bear in the actual conversation you have with the students. Note that my emphasis is not on you the instructor, but on your students. You can get to know them, understand where they are in relation to the materials, and concentrate on meeting their needs as learners. The materials provided are just the jumping-off point, not the ending point. I teach the occasional course as well as being a faculty trainer, and—here I thought it safe to suggest something not really approved, but c'mon, they can't really mean that, can they?—I sometimes provide links to outside resources that flat out contradict the provided readings. In the ensuing conversation with the students, we end up covering much important ground on the nature of history and the role of the historian.

This advice seemed good enough and not likely to cause comment, but I later realized that all it would take for this faculty member to lose her job, if she followed it, would be for a student to mention to a staff member at the university that the instructor had gone off-script. This is the *business* of online education, and the point is not so much the creation of educated students, though that may be a happy bonus. It is instead the extraction of money as efficiently as possible. Anything that interferes with this is to be eliminated. I sat in on a meeting where the several hundred recruiters for the university were getting a pep talk from the CEO. Or maybe "pep talk" is too innocuous. It had the air of a partisan election rally, complete with chants and cheering. The CEO said words to the effect of, "You need to keep a student in a class if we're going to make a profit! And if a faculty member is causing trouble, you let us know, and that faculty member is out! Keep the students enrolled at all costs!" Then we saw the matrix, the grid upon which all faculty members were scored, and how they kept or lost their jobs. Much cheering. Faculty were the enemy. Off-script faculty were the worst.

That advice I offered? That slightly-off-script advice? It turns out, my colleagues were similarly gently pushing against the system we were in. Our actions had been noted, over time, and as a result, our ability to work remotely was removed. Henceforth, the work would happen at the main call center, under closer supervision. Move to Arizona if you want to keep your job.

What kind of failure is this? There were certainly many opportunities to reflect on what I now recognize as the Type 1 and Type 2 failures in the day-to-day operations of the university. I learned that an enormous toll is taken on what are considered best practices in online education when it is scaled up as fast and at such scale as we did, because the only way to survive (as a student, as an instructor, as a staff member) is to be the kind of human that the machine imagines. Roopika Risam notes this exact issue in her book *New Digital Worlds*, wherein she discusses that the digital humanities should be exploring the kind of human imagined by the technologies, the systems, that we create (136). When I look at the experience from the perspective of a Type 3 failure, I see how the churn, the turnover, the sheer human waste that the system depended on was not a bug, but rather a feature of the system: *it was working as designed, for the purpose of making money.* Disillusioning. Tressie McMillam Cottom explores the sociology of the for-profit education scene in her brilliant work *Lower Ed*, drawing on her own experience working in this sector. What is digital humanities for, if not for doing the work that Risam and McMillam Cottom are doing? Teaching online is not digital humanities; filtering that teaching through (for instance) this fail framework, and reflecting on the systemic impacts that it has ... perhaps that is digital humanities. And though I didn't know the label yet, it was in that frame of mind that I saw the advertisement for the digital humanities job at Carleton University just as our department was getting wound down.

Part Two

Getting Over Myself

That was always the dream, wasn't it? "I wish I knew then what I know now"? But when you got older, you found out that you now wasn't you then. You then was a twerp. You then was what you had to be to start out on the rocky road of becoming you now, and one of the rocky patches on that road was being a twerp. (Terry Pratchett, *Night Watch*)

In this section, I put aside the fail framework for a moment. Instead, I want to focus on some of the human and humane issues that were present in the last section—empathy or its lack; churn and disillusionment; impact and connection—and recognize that, while all of these might fit under the Type 2 rubric, they require a deeper engagement.

Which brings us to twerps. Pratchett, as ever, hits the nail on the head with gentle comedy. *Night Watch* is a police procedural with a time-traveling twist, and so becomes a rumination on how it is that we become the persons we are. In it, policeman Sam Vimes from the future takes on the training of Sam Vimes from the past, and looks with dismay at the road his younger self is about to travel.

The passage resonates, for I was a twerp. In grad school and the years to follow, there were things I needed to learn the hard way. The actual stories of how I came to experience these lessons are frankly too much, too painful, to tell you. Failing in public has its limits, after all. In this section instead I tell small stories that capture some of what I think was missing from my character, my approach, *my teaching*, as I moved from job to job, situation to situation. We have to start with ourselves, if we are eventually going to be able to fail gloriously; sometimes, we only spot that we were twerps afterward because the others around us did the emotional labor of keeping us safe. Shielding us, as it were, from our twerpiness.

The Man at the Door

The doorbell rang; the man standing there looked like he might be in his late fifties. Tall, strong, his wife and son in tow. He asked for my dad.

"You might not remember me, but I worked for you in the summers when I was a kid, on your farm. I rolled a load of hay, once. My name is . . . "

My mom and dad welcomed them in, and over the next hour, it was the early 1970s again. Old names, "Do you remember . . .," directions past landmarks that no longer exist. Coffee made, poured, drunk. Stories told. The perils of McCormack tractors, the difficulties of getting to town in those days. This man's father had bought my great-grandfather's farm, and for a year or so, had the best days of his life—his words. (Years later, one of my own graduate students would grow up, for a time, on that same farm, but that's a story for another day.)

It was a pleasant visit, but it left my folks a little bemused. Forty years is a long time, and as they say, another country. But I could tell my dad was pleased. After all, of all the things this fellow and his family could've been doing that day, they sought out my dad. For whatever reason, it was important for this fellow to find my dad and tell him that working for him was one of the best experiences he'd ever had.

My dad has farmed, he's milled feed, he's delivered pails of fuel to folks in the middle of the night to keep their furnace on in the dead of winter, he's pressed apples to make cider. He's made his own work for himself, worked for other people, and provided work for many more. He's been a quiet supporter of this village, this place, its people, all his life. It's a family joke that we could be in the middle of Italy and he'd still run into someone he knows. He's the kind of guy who knows everyone—or if he doesn't, he soon will. He's a man who's made a difference, in his quiet way. The visit left me thinking—am I doing anything that'll cause someone to seek me out in thirty years, just to chat, to introduce me to their family?

This man sought out my dad because at a point in his life when he needed it, my dad stepped up and did the work. It wasn't glamorous work, it wasn't work with the expectation of reward. And if no one had stepped up, what would have happened? Did my dad even recognize that it was work? I think, if I had asked him, he'd only be embarrassed and would just shrug his shoulders and give a half-smile.

But it is work, and we need to see it for what it is. Because we don't or won't see it or recognize it even when we're doing it, we don't recognize it in others. The burden falls elsewhere. Aimée Morrison writes about having to do the care work of five other professors and how it's burning her out in a blog post entitled "If Not You, Then Who?":

> "I don't think students get through a degree without some extensions, without crying in someone's office sometimes, without needing something explained in great detail, one on one, without mentoring and advising, without meaningful interpersonal contact. And if that's true, then *someone* is always doing that labour. And I can say for certain that it's not everyone and I have deep suspicions that there is a strong gender and disciplinary factor in who actually is doing this work."

This care-work can be a source of joy though, when we take on our share of it. The man who came to visit didn't seek out my dad because he put himself out there. Dad just is. It's how he's chosen to move through life. You can make this choice too:

Don't be a jerk.

Treat people with generosity.

Don't accept bullshit from others, but err on the side of believing the best of them.

Do the work that sets other people up for success.

That's all it takes. This is part of the job. Yet it still seems it's surprisingly hard to do. It's the emotional labor of our work, and it is the labor that disproportionately falls on women, on contingent faculty, on early career scholars, on the people with the least amount of time and security to do the work. By abdicating this responsibility, by pushing the labor onto those least able to say no, we compound the sense of not belonging, of imposter syndrome. And this disparity leads to fewer opportunities for others, fewer role models, and burnout.

Will there be a knock on your door?

Mashed Potatoes

"Do it again. Top of the page."

"Again."

"Again. You mumbled those last lines."

"Again."

I remember Gramma sitting on the couch with my copy of the script. The high school play was in a few weeks. I hadn't learned my lines, so there she was, taking on the task. Coaching me. Cajoling me. Pushing me. Over and over, until I got it right. Nearly ten years later in 2001, I was sitting in her living room again, but this time she had a draft of my PhD in front of her.

"Why do you say this on page forty? Explain that to me again."

"No. That made no sense. You said it was completely different, three pages before."

"No, you can't have a cookie, not until you tell me why this part matters."

If the thesis made any sense, it was in large part due to that same coaching. Questioning. Cajoling.

In 2019, my brother handed me a cassette tape. It's labeled, "Interview with Gramma, 1994." It was part of the research for *his* MA thesis, a local history. Gramma passed away two months after I got my PhD. I haven't heard her voice since I sat with her in her hospital room in December 2002 and proudly showed her my diploma (I was home for a brief visit, glowing in the success of getting my PhD, and about to start—I thought—a career). The cassette sat in my hand, and my brother and I stared at it. "I haven't tried to play it, he said. "I thought maybe the machine would eat it, and anyway, I figured you'd know some digital way to get the sound off it."

I haven't tried to play it yet. I can hear her voice in my head though: "Well? Get on with it!" And then she laughs.

Gramma was a major fixture in my life growing up. She was a teacher; from the Eastern Townships of Quebec she'd moved to our region fresh out of teacher's college in Montreal. She had won a scholarship to Bishops University to study math in the 1920s, but the university had no women's dorm. Her father overruled her and sent her to Montreal instead, where the college did have a women's dorm. "Y'know," she once said, after making me explain my latest thesis research to her satisfaction, "I think I would've quite liked to do what you're doing."

I'm grateful for everything that Gramma did for me, but at the same time, dragging the best out of me was work for her. It seems that sometimes a person can become accustomed to expecting someone else's labor as a necessary and rightful part of their own work. Doesn't there come a point where I should be capable of doing this on my own? Some of us never reach it.

I perhaps reached that watershed not through any positive decision or realization of what I was doing, but when my relationship with my partner at the time (and that had sustained me through the PhD) finally broke down. The social network that went with that relationship did not last either, and finally, I was entirely alone. It is not uncommon to speak of emotional labor in the context of working at a university—the unsung meetings with students, the writing of reference letters, the service on another damned committee, supporting others' students on *just this one thing can you help me it won't take too long can't you teach me*? But there's also the emotional labor of our partners, friends, and families to enable us to *be* this thing, an academic. All of these things take a toll on our emotional intelligence, our emotional health, our connections to each other. Sometimes, it is exhausted. Sometimes, you cause a lot of damage.

I don't know whether Gramma would ever have regarded these things as labor, but I do know that if you didn't say "thank you," acknowledge it, and return it in kind, you'd soon have cause for regret. My father treats people with generosity, and this is a kind of emotional labor, too. The system that we are working in, this system that does not tolerate failure, is a fundamentally ungenerous system that runs on emotional labor. I tried to work within its rules, and I was ungenerous. I relied upon, unthinkingly, others' emotional labor. Emotional labor is necessary, but it is not equally distributed. Those who exhibit generosity, who try to be open and present, too often are depleted and exhausted. What to do?

Jo Van Every, an academic and coach, has very good advice for ways to deal with the demands of emotional labor: "Don't Do Your Best." By this she means identify the important parts of the work and only do the minimum, the truly important bits. That is to say: don't accept others' bullshit. One night at dinner, so the story goes, Grandpa was going on and on about something in the newspaper, giving his opinion at length to the table. Gramma said, "Pass the mashed potatoes, please." She then loaded up her spoon, pulled back, and launched, hitting Grandpa on the nose.

Sometimes, you have to throw potatoes. Gramma didn't argue, didn't try to convince Grandpa of the merits of some other point of view. Gramma just decided that she'd had enough. When it's time to throw the potatoes, throw 'em hard.

The Wake

It was de Polignac, I think, who wrote about the meaning of the great Panathenaic Festival. Whereas other cities of classical Greece had urban and rural sanctuaries, Athens had only the urban. And so, while other cities' citizens would proceed out to the rural sanctuaries for their festivals, Athens' great procession wound through its streets and open spaces: a show by the city, for the city; a demonstration of the city's character and foundation stories to itself. Through the procession, the city reaffirmed its character and that of its citizens.

Something like that, anyway. It's been a while since I've read de Polignac.

A similar impulse lay behind the Romans' salutatio and procession to the forum. It was a game of seeing and being seen. I suppose it's all a form of costly signaling at a societal level—a way of reinscribing a sense of who "we" are, whomever we may be, by showing us to ourselves.

I was thinking about all this as I stood outside a funeral home recently, taking my place at the end of the queue to pay my respects. Wakes are funny things. Irish wakes, so I've always been told, are moments of communal drinking, singing, and carousing, a celebration that the rest of us are still alive. Which makes me think of the funeral games of the ancient epic.

This was not that kind of wake. In Shawville, the heritage is a dour Northern Irish Protestantism, a Quebec town with seven churches, none of them Catholic. A Shawville wake works like this. On the other side of the entrance to the funeral home lies a long rectangular room, with the entrance on the one corner. Across the diagonal lies the deceased, surrounded by flowers. The family of the deceased is arranged in a receiving line. The spouse will stand beside the casket, with children and their spouses/children to the left so that the youngest will be encountered first by the people in the queue. Cousins, in-laws, and other family members will be to the right. Mourners enter the room and turn to the right along the one long wall. Often there is a little shrine of photographs or (more recently) a PowerPoint presentation set up there. The first person in the queue shakes the hand of the first family member. After a brief murmur of words, they will step over to the next family member. The queue will move in fits and starts as each person has a moment to pay their respects to each member of the family, stopping quietly in front of the casket before moving on.

The circuit of the room concludes with the signing of the book of condolences, followed by an exit down the street. Often the queue extends out the door to the corner or beyond. During one's time in the queue, one will hear murmurs of "Good turnout," or "There's Susan, doesn't she live in the city now?" or "Who's that with John, is that the new wife?" or "Didn't you go to school with so-and-so? There they are!"

The wake functions, for Shawville, like the ancient processions of Athens and Rome. The wake surfaces the connections of obligation or respect that normally are too diffuse to spot. The wake is a clotting factor. Every wake is also an opportunity for the community to remember who it is and how it got there. My brother is a full-time faculty member at the high school and lives in this community. He was about two dozen people ahead of me in the line. Almost every person leaving the wake spoke to him or nodded their heads in greeting as they passed. He has to go to a lot of these things, my brother. A teacher in a small community is a node in nearly all social networks, in nearly all social gatherings. Every year, one or two students (or former students) are killed. Farming accident. Hunting accident. Road accident. Overdose. Sickness. He goes to them all.

He goes to the wakes of students' parents and grandparents. He goes to the wakes of people he grew up with. He goes to the wakes of families connected to ours. He goes, and does what needs to be done. He's there to show respect, but also, because he understands his role.

I probably see more students in a year than he does, but I don't know them in any meaningful way. One or two, some of the MA or other grad students, maybe. I am fundamentally disconnected in a way almost diametrically opposite to the way he is connected. At the wake, his connectedness is apparent. But that's just the sad flipside to the wonder of his connectedness to his students. The wonderful aspect shows in his everyday interactions with his students, with their families, with the community. It makes a difference for these students to have that connection. If that aspect didn't exist, he would not be there at the wake, waiting his turn.

What would it take for me to have that kind of connection with my students? The reader might feel that there's an irony here: *see the digital guy worrying about connecting!* What kind of connection could be possible in a way that fairly spreads the emotional labor? It's a question worth asking though, because to some, the answer is **MOAR data!** Datafication. Tracking. Surveillance masking as engagement analytics. Surveillance masking as care. None of these things lead to community like that at the wake. They are instead the antithesis of community.

The things that are easy to measure gain their importance in that they are the things easy to measure, but they are not necessarily the meaningful things. The words of condolence spoken at a wake; the shared memory eliciting a quiet chuckle; the impact of seeing an entire community turn out to pay its respects; the cascades of affect and the sense of being valued that travels through the social networks on display: these things are not able to be measured in any way that would not diminish them.

The wake shows us to ourselves and brings what matters to the fore. When the Taylorists and the Trumpists come for the universities, it will only be the connections we've forged, the actual community we've built, the generosity of spirit in setting others up for success, that will save us. What have you done lately to merit mention at the wake?

Rock of Ages

I'm not one for public crying, but tears were streaming down my face as I was stopped at the intersection of Hunt Club and Prince of Wales. I caught the eye of the woman in the car next to me, and she turned away.

I had been stuck in traffic, idly flipping between the radio stations. Alt rock. Classic Rock. Best of the 60s, 70s, and 80s! The CBC. NPR, floating in over the border. Then I hit the media button for the CD player by accident, and the voice of Stuart McLean embraced me.

Stuart McLean died of cancer in 2015. He was many things over the years, but first and foremost, he was a storyteller. His Vinyl Cafe stories played on the radio every Saturday. They were funny, warm, and often poignant, insights into the life of his everyman, Dave, and Dave's wider community. The story that was playing in my car was called "Rock of Ages." It's a story of an old woman from Dave's hometown who, for reasons she can't explain, passes up a chance to reconnect with an old beau. He dies not long after, and at the funeral, she sings "Rock of Ages." But of course, in the recording, it is Stuart McLean who is singing. In that instant, I am transported back to my childhood, to our rural church, and I'm thinking of the people I will never see again. I'm thinking of Gramma.

And I cried.

I saw Stuart McLean twice in concert for his Christmas show in Ottawa. The National Art Centre squats in downtown Ottawa beside the Rideau Canal. Inside, despite the vast space, it feels close, intimate. On the stage there is a stand-up microphone.

A wingback chair is stage left. And that is all. Stuart walks onto the stage and, once the applause settles down, he begins to speak.

It is a masterclass in speaking. I am enthralled. It's not just the richness of the voice, or the humor, pacing, and timing, though those are all impeccable. It's the physicality. He holds his head perfectly still as he tells the story, reading from his script propped up on the music stand. But the rest of his body—his arms windmill; his legs noodle forward and backward; his hands splay and grasp and point. He is conducting an orchestra, juggling the lives of Dave, Morely, Sam, Arthur the dog, the minor characters, the walk-ons. But throughout, he holds his head steady. His voice never betrays the maelstrom happening just underneath. And after a while it becomes clear that the movement, all the movement, is Stuart McLean moving through his own palace of memory. He has the script in front of him, but his eyes are closed. He can *see* Dave, there, about to turn on the dryer into which the pet ferret has crept; he's *there* in the kitchen when Dave decides to do a spot of remodeling.

This I think was the secret to Stuart McLean's success. He is present in his work in a way few of us ever are. Even as I listen to the old CD, I can see him windmilling away as Dave tries to shepherd the boys onto the subway, the subway doors closing in his face. And sometimes, I can see him holding himself very still and trying to contain that energy in his slight frame, like when he sings "Rock of Ages." Stillness is so much more effective when it is unexpected. This is what I aspire to. To be present in the moment when I lecture, when I speak. To be still in the center of that moment. To move and be moved in turn.

This past year, I was responsible for organizing the department's speaker series, and I wanted to make space to discuss some of the failures of our discipline. The theme was "bad archaeology," that is, the ways archaeological knowledge can be ill-used or go wrong. The speakers were from all career stages, both within and outside of formal academia. In their own individual ways, the speakers had that same emotional affect, that stillness in the center of the moment, that drove the message home. As each spoke about the fails they had experienced in archaeology and the larger issues in the field as a whole, I was able to witness the cumulative impact they had on my students who attended each talk. Kisha Supernant of the University of Alberta, in particular, discussed how her training in archaeological GIS and a scientific approach to archaeology conflicted with her engagement with her own Métis heritage. It was a story of connection to community, of emotional labor, of the conflicting demands of the systems we are in and the humanity we need in our work. Her storytelling was profound, kind, and generous, and it enabled us to see what she was seeing. She was present in the work, and so made the work present in her listeners. This is what I aspire to.

Part Three

Fits and Starts and Fumbles

Ok. This is it. There's this job. I can do this. It's *me*. It's so me. How do I start?

Research the department. What do they do? Anyone working in what I do? No? Anything adjacent? Who could I work with, who would I collaborate with?

What did they say in their advertisement—what does it sound like they're looking for? What's unsaid? What's reinforced? What do I do that fits with that? What could I teach, what could I research, and where would these fit into their programs? What could I do that would make things *even better*?

How does what I do fit into the broader field? How does my work move the field forward? What do they need to know about what I do? What impact have I already had?

What would being a part of their department do for me as a scholar, as a teacher? What are my strengths, what are my weaknesses, how do I fit into their puzzle? How do they fit *with me*? How would I work with students? How would students work with me?

Arrange this into a story. Make it so that it's easy for them to imagine seeing me walking around the place. Let it be obvious. The letter is not my CV. My CV is my CV. The letter is me changing the world so that there's a Shawn-shaped space in their heads. Tell the story cleanly. Tell the story without hyperbole. Tell the *story*. Show it to people. Lots of people. People I trust. Who do I trust?

Practice telling the story. The mock lecture—that's me telling the story for undergrads. Practice it. Practice.

Alright. This is it. I can do this.

Click "send."

There was a crack in the door, a chink in the wall, a stone that you could get a toehold on, a rope dangling *just there*. And now, imposter that you are, you are standing in the hallway of this university department, the very first day, all alone.

Now what?

You're an expert on this one particular thing (at least, so you've convinced them). You could do just about anything, with the kind of self-discipline you've learned. After all, you found a question, you figured out how to solve the question, you went out and solved the damned thing. You could do just about anything, with a mind like that.

But.

We also convinced you that there's only one kind of thing you can do, at least in the humanities. And we made the rest of the world think that's all you can do, too. We've really screwed things up there.

You just might get hired for your research, for that one job we've convinced everyone you're a good fit for because of your degree. But you'll keep that job because of your teaching. And we didn't teach you how to teach. If you get good at the teaching, we'll promote you to some other job that we haven't trained you for, either. We've set you up to feel like an imposter for the rest of your days.

It's hard not to be cynical. At one point, I didn't even include my PhD on my CV, because I'd been turned down for too many jobs. There were occasional bright spots. I answered a classified advertisement looking for a researcher. A contractor wanted to know what the laws and regulations were in order to build a retirement home. I did not expect much success, because I'd heard the terrible litany too many times already:

"You're over qualified."

"You'd never stay."

"You'd never be happy here."

What turned it around was remembering that I was a storyteller. There are many stories in the world that shape people's thinking; equating a PhD with fitness for academia only is a very strong one (and one that academics have brought upon themselves). This time, I tried telling a different story. I walked into the interview with part of the web of regulations already mapped out. "Finding the regulations is only one part of the job you want done. The other part is understanding the context of those regulations, how they are interpreted in the world. I can provide that context: that's a core part of how I approach the world."

How do you get started? You tell a story. You, not the CV. Not the degree. Not the articles or projects. You take what you can do, you meet people where they are, and you shape what you do into the available space in other people's heads. You shape that space into a you-shaped hole.

In Fits and Starts and Fumbles, I tell the story of getting started as this thing, the digital humanities guy in the History department. Getting that toehold, squeezing through the narrow door—that required one kind of story. But when you're actually on the job, in a role you never thought existed, for something you didn't train to do and aren't entirely convinced that you can do, that you certainly don't know how to teach and nobody else around you does either (in fact, they're expecting you to show them)—that's something very different.

I did not have a framework for failing gloriously at that time. I had a nebulous sense that the only time I actually learned how to do something, or learned why something mattered, was when I did it in public, on the web, within the context of a larger sympathetic group.

Once, in the course of my PhD research on Roman brick stamps, I decided that I would really like to see in action how bricks were made. If I understood the context of how these things came to be, perhaps I would understand better the patterns that I was mapping out in the associated clays and their distribution. What I wanted, in fact, was some experimental archaeology.

We traveled to the Ironbridge Gorge in Shropshire, England, where there was a traditional brickmaker's meetup. We parked the car along the narrow road and walked to the gnarly old oak tree where we were supposed to meet the brickmakers. We could smell the smoke from the kiln, and there in a clearing in the woods, we found not just the kiln, but a community with its own rhythms and habits that emerged at the intersection of the requirements of wood and clay and ingenuity. We spent the day looking at the different clays, the forms, the ways in which a kiln could be built and how it would affect the draft, the dispersal of heat, the differences between permanent kilns and clamp kilns, the thoroughness with which a brick might be fired or not depending on its positioning inside. When I wanted precise answers, the folks there merely laughed and suggested rules of thumb. What was unclear to me when looking at artifacts alone made sense when I saw the same materials taking shape within the group, those materials then shaping the group in turn.

Digital work, I've learned, is very similar. We come to it full of anxiety about the precision of the machine, and the systems and rules within things have to work. We want precise answers, but there are really just answers "good enough for now." With time, it turns out that the only way to get anything done is to say "This isn't working, what do you folks think?" We have to develop an ability to understand that everything is always broken. We shape the work, but the work, the tech, shapes us, too.

Easy to say now. In "How I Lost the Crowd," I reproduce a slightly edited version of the blog post from 2012, two years into this digital humanities thing, detailing the death of my HeritageCrowd platform: a very public, very excruciating fail. I have added a postscript to it categorizing the ways in which it failed in terms of the "Failing Gloriously" framework. The next piece, "Research Witchcraft," is a blog post from two years later that is expanded on. In it, you can see that I'm starting to fumble toward what Croxall and Warnick codify in their types of fails. "Research Witchcraft" also gestures toward the way the work of the digital humanities, digital archaeology, and digital history are allied to the habits of thought that researchers in the world of experimental archaeology enjoy. The last three pieces turn back to my students during this period, to consider how unsettling this way of work is and why making it safe to fail has to be part of failing gloriously. That it involves, as per Quinn Dombrowski, doing right by others. I recount two cases of emotional labor in which I had the opportunity to be generous, to do right, but with mixed results.

How I Lost the Crowd

In 2010 I became the digital humanities guy. As part of my startup package, I received a small grant. I used it to hire Nadine and Guy, and we began a project that used the Ushahidi crisis-mapping platform—a content management system that allowed people to text, phone, or email reports during a crisis, which were then mapped and categorized—as a venue to map the intangible heritage of Renfrew and Pontiac Counties in Eastern Ontario and Western Quebec. Instead of reporting 'power lines down!' people could report 'there used to be a...' The idea was that people could phone, text, or email their stories about the heritage of their community and then by mapping it, we would validate that knowledge and enable sharing and deeper stories to emerge. That was the idea, at any rate. If you leave your front door open, can you be upset if vandals walk in? And so, in the early summer of 2012, the site was corrupted. I wrote this in the immediate aftermath.

Yesterday, my HeritageCrowd project website was annihilated. Gone. Kaputt. Destroyed. Joined the choir.

It is a dead parrot.

This is what I think happened, what I now know and need to learn, and what I think the wider digital humanities community needs to think about/teach each other.

HeritageCrowd was (and may be again, if I can salvage the wreckage) a project that tried to encourage the crowdsourcing of local cultural heritage knowledge for a community that does not have particularly good internet access or penetration. It was built on the Ushahidi platform, which allows folks to participate via cellphone text messages. We even had it set up so that a person could leave a voice message and software would automatically transcribe the message and submit it via email. It worked fairly well, and we wrote it up for *Writing History in the Digital Age* (which also detailed our surprise at how some communities used the perceived authority of the site—it being a university project, after all—in local planning politics). I was looking forward to working more on it this summer.

> **Problem #1:** Poor recordkeeping of the process of getting things installed and the decisions taken.

Now originally, we were using the Crowdmap-hosted version of Ushahidi rather than installing the full platform ourselves, so we wouldn't have to worry about things like security, updates, servers, that sort of thing. But I wanted to customize the look, move the content blocks around, and make some other cosmetic changes so that Ushahidi's genesis in crisis mapping wouldn't be quite as evident. When you repurpose software meant for one domain to another, it's the sort of thing you do. So, I set up a new domain, got some server space, downloaded Ushahidi, and installed it. The installation tested my server skills. Unlike setting up WordPress or Omeka (which I've done several times), Ushahidi requires the concomitant set up of Kohana, a web framework for building PHP-powered sites. This was not easy. There are many levels of tacit knowledge in computing and especially in web-based applications that I, as an outsider, have not yet learned. It takes a lot of trial and error and sometimes, just dumb luck. I kept poor records of this period—I was working with a tight deadline, and I wanted to just get the damned thing working. Today, I have no idea what I actually did to get Kohana and Ushahidi playing nicely with one another. I think it actually boiled down to file structure.

(It's funny to think of myself as an outsider when it comes to all this digital work. I am, after all, an official, card-carrying digital humanist. It's worth remembering what that label actually means. I spent well over a decade learning how to do the humanist part. I've only been at the digital part since about 2005, and my experience with digital, at least initially, was in social networks and simulation—things that don't actually require me to mount materials on the internet. We forget sometimes that there's more to the digital humanities than building flashy internet-based digital tools).

Problem #2: Computers talk to other computers and persuade them to do things.

I forget where I read it now (it was probably Stephen Ramsay or Geoffrey Rockwell), but digital humanists need to consider artificial intelligence. We do a humanities not just of other humans, but of humans' creations that engage in their own goal-directed behaviors. As someone who has built a number of agent-based models and simulations, I suppose I shouldn't have forgotten this. But on the internet, there is a whole netherworld of computers corrupting each other for all sorts of purposes.

HeritageCrowd was destroyed so that one computer could persuade another computer to send spam to gullible humans with erectile dysfunction. Its database was filled with spam, and then the code that would normally have served the site became corrupted and tasked with sending that spam out into the world.

Apparently the version of Ushahidi that I installed was vulnerable to cross-site request forgery (CSRF) and cross-site scripting (XSS) attacks. I think that what happened to HeritageCrowd was an instance of persistent XSS:

The persistent (or stored) XSS vulnerability is a more devastating variant of a cross-site scripting flaw: it occurs when the data provided by the attacker is saved by the server, and then permanently displayed on "normal" pages returned to other users in the course of regular browsing, without proper HTML escaping. – Wikipedia, "Cross-site scripting"

When I examine every PHP file on the site, there are all sorts of injected base64 code (strings of letters and numbers that to a human are unintelligible but are in fact encoded instructions). So this is what killed my site. Once my site started flooding spam all over the place, the internet's immune systems (my host's own, and others) shut it all down. Now, I could just clean everything out and reinstall, but there's a more devastating issue: it appears my SQL database containing the stories and cultural heritage materials is gone. Destroyed. Erased. No longer present. I've asked my host to help confirm that, because at this point, I'm way out of my league. Hey all you lone digital humanists: how often does your computing services department help you out in this regard? Find someone at your institution who can handle this kind of thing. We can't wear every hat.

Problem #3: Security Warnings

There are many Ushahidi installations all over the world, and they deal with some pretty sensitive stuff. Security is therefore something Ushahidi takes seriously. I should've too. I was not subscribed to the Ushahidi Security Advisories. The hardest pill to swallow is when you know it's your own damned fault. The warnings were there; heed the warnings! Schedule time into every week to keep on top of security. If you've got a team, task someone to look after this. I have lots of excuses—it was end of term, things were due, meetings to be held, grades to get in—but it was my responsibility. And I dropped the ball.

Problem #4: Backups

This is the most embarrassing thing to admit. I did not back things up regularly. I am not ever making that mistake again. Over on Looted Heritage (my project that monitors the news media for stories about the antiquities trade, which also uses the hosted always-up-to-date-security-wise version of Ushahidi), I have an if-this-then-that (ifttt.com) recipe set up that sends every new report to BufferApp, which then tweets it. I've also got one that sends every report to Evernote. There are probably more elegant ways to do this, and Twitter and Evernote are certainly not backing things up. But the worst would be to remind myself to manually download things. That didn't work the first time. It ain't gonna work the next.

[*Shawn in 2019 looks back at Shawn from 2012 and says, oh nooooooo none of this is good at all!*]

So what do I do now?

If I can get my database back, I'll clean everything out and reinstall, and then progress onward, wiser for the experience. If I can't . . . well, perhaps that's the end of HeritageCrowd. It was always an experiment, and as Scott Weingart reminds us in 'Halting Conditions':

> The best we can do is not as much as we can, but as much as we need. There is a point of diminishing return for data collection; that point at which you can't measure the coastline fast enough before the tides change it. We as humanists have to become comfortable with incompleteness and imperfection, and trust that in aggregate those data can still tell us something, even if they can't reveal everything. (2012)

The HeritageCrowd project taught me quite a lot about crowdsourcing cultural heritage, about building communities, about the problems, potentials, and perils of data management. Even in its (quite probable) death, I've learned some hard lessons. I share them here so that you don't have to make the same mistakes. Make new ones! Share them! The next time I go to THATCamp, I know what I'll be proposing. I want a session on the black hats and the dark side of the force. I want to know what the resources are for learning how they work, what I can do to protect myself, and frankly, more about the social and cultural anthropology of their world. Perhaps there is space in the digital humanities for that.

P.S.

When I discovered what had happened, I tweeted about it. Thank you everyone who responded with help and advice. That's the final lesson about this episode, I think. Don't be afraid to share your failures and ask for help. As Bethany Nowviskie wrote some time ago, we're at that point where we're building the new ways of knowing for the future, just like the Lunaticks in the eighteenth century. Embrace your inner Lunatick:

> Those 18th-century Lunaticks weren't about the really big theories and breakthroughs— instead, their heroic work was to codify knowledge, found professional societies and journals, and build all the enabling infrastructure that benefited a succeeding generation of scholars and scientists. [. . .] if you agree with me that there's something remarkable about a generation of trained scholars ready to subsume themselves in collaborative endeavours, to do the grunt work, and to step back from the podium into roles only they can

play—that is, to become systems-builders for the humanities—then we might also just pause to appreciate and celebrate, and to use "#alt-ac" as a safe place for people to say, "I'm a Lunatick, too."

Perhaps my role is to fail gloriously and often, so you don't have to. I'm ok with that.

Let's reexamine this piece within the framework established for failing gloriously.

Problems #1 and #3 are human fails (Type 2) in that I didn't fully understand the implications of the choices I was making. It might not be necessary to understand absolutely everything that goes on in the code as long as you understand the context and implications of the choices you are making. Problems #2 and #4 are arguably technical fails (perhaps Problem #4 is also a human fail). The post as a whole moves us into the realm of a Type 3 fail, where we consider what happened as a kind of artifact, while the postscript moves us toward fail-as-epistemology.

Failing gloriously, as I wrote in the introduction, has a few dimensions. To fail gloriously is to embrace the freedom that being an imposter can give, to tinker, to break things, to imagine how things could be different, and to make it safe for others to do the same.

Even though it was not a conscious thing, I think that I felt, pre-tenure, that posting this post-mortem might speak to the freedom of being an imposter: no one knew what the job was supposed to do, so who's to say it *wasn't* about breaking things and reporting back? Does this post make it safe for others to do that? It does, I think, in that it lets sunlight in on the messiness of doing digital work. Social norms do not come out of nowhere. To normalize something, we have to see it in action every day. And hopefully, it becomes safer for others who do not have our privilege to do it, too.

Does this post imagine how things could be different? That is to say, does it address some of the more fundamental systemic issues at play given the context of the work? This post might have been the first time I used the phrase "fail gloriously" in a way that leads directly to this present volume. It is clear that the impetus for thinking along these lines is the work and research of Bethany Nowviskie. But the rest of the piece is ungenerous in who it cites. As Sharon Leon points out in "Returning Women to the History of Digital History," the history of digital history is replete with individuals doing innovative, experimental work out in the open that I could have drawn on as I wrote my post-mortem. That I didn't know the field is no excuse: is it not my job to find out? In this, the piece is not imagining a different possibility space but merely replicating the existing order. Indeed, when Ian Milligan, Scott Weingart, and I began writing the manuscript for *The Historian's Macroscope*, we managed to do it *again*. Recognizing at the last moment what we had done, we published a final essay on our supporting website (themacroscope.org) just as that book was going to press:

> While it is impossible for any single book to exhaustively cover digital history, a few vital subjects did not make it into the final draft. We regretfully neglected explicit discussions of **diversity and equality,** subjects we feel **should play a role in every digital historian's training.** [. . .] we tried to de-centre ourselves and write a book that not only taught digital history methods, but embodied the kinds of perspectives that we consider integral to good digital history. Nevertheless, upon inspecting our content in the months before its

release, we discovered lacunae we regret. Recent research on digital humanities practices opened our eyes to how gendered the topical landscape of DH still is, and to the significant barriers to diversity still present among digital humanists.

On a similar note, citation is a gift, as Jules Weiss wrote:

> "Real punks consider whose voices are being heard, when, and why, and they take action to uplift the voices of those who are often spoken over. [. . .] We can punk citation [. . .] by making citation into an act of accomplice-ship instead of accomplishment-making."

I will return to this thought in the final section, on what digital humanities could be when framed through the lens of glorious failure. In the imperative to think about how things could be different and to do things differently, maybe it draws on a punk sensibility. For now, "How I Lost the Crowd" is almost, but not quite, a glorious failure.

Research Witchcraft

I'm starting out. I'm the digital guy. I'm an imposter. People keep asking me questions. I can't answer them. I'm going to be found out. The one digital thing I know how to do—build agent-based models in the Netlogo environment—doesn't translate well into the world I now find myself in, since digital historians don't *do* agent models. What's more, I took a course in building models, a one-week workshop some five years ago. Someone sat down and worked out a curriculum and exercises towards a very constrained goal: how to use this program, this environment, to do one kind of thing. Transferable knowledge only in the broadest terms, I think. I'm sometimes out of my depth.

I'm also a fan of Terry Pratchett. I reread his novels frequently because each time, I find something new to consider. I was recently reading *Lords and Ladies*, which is part of the witches' cycle of stories set in Discworld. This passage resonated:

> Cottages tend to attract similar kinds of witches. It's natural. Every witch trains up one or two young witches in their life, and when in the course of mortal time the cottage becomes vacant it's only sense for one of them to move in.
>
> Magrat's cottage traditionally housed thoughtful witches who noticed things and wrote things down. Which herbs were better than others for headaches, fragments of old stories, odds and ends like that. [...]
>
> It was a cottage of questioning witches, research witches. Eye of what newt? What species of ravined salt-sea shark? It's all very well a potion calling for

Love-in-idleness, but which of the thirty-seven common plants called by that name in various parts of the continent was actually meant?

The reason that Granny Weatherwax was a better witch than Magrat was that she knew that in witchcraft it didn't matter a damn which one it was, or even if it was a piece of grass.

The reason that Magrat was a better doctor than Granny was that she thought it did. (Pratchett 1992: 166)

A lot of the tools that digital historians or digital archaeologists use are shared as open-source software, often using the services of code repositories such as Github.com. Take a look at any GitHub repository, any package contained there, and examine the readme file. Readme files are by convention the place where installation instructions, lists of dependencies, example usages, and so on are detailed. To me, there's a lot of the witches about these code repositories. The parallel isn't perfect, but I feel rather like poor Magrat. For instance, here is what one taken-at-random readme file says about a particular package:

- Install PostgreSQL.
- Install JDK.
- Git clone repo.

What's a JDK? Oh, Java Development Kit. Wait, what version of JDK? How many flavors of PostgreSQL are there? Git? What do I do with that? Whenever I install something, there's always something else that has to be installed first. But what? And how?

As I fumble toward dim understanding, I figure the folks who are building these things are more like Granny and understand that any development kit will do the trick, because they know what to expect and how to fix it if it goes wrong. Me, I need the right version the first time, because otherwise I'll just make a hash of it—and I'll have to teach it to someone!

I don't have the tacit knowledge of experience built up yet, those things that Granny knows in her bones and doesn't have to explain. There's just so much to learn! Like Magrat, I can write it all down, spell it all out, and in doing so, I'll eventually become like Granny.

I look forward to that day. But for now, I'll keep engaging in my research witchcraft, figuring out the bits and bobs that those far more clever than me have devised and then reporting back what I've discovered.

I haven't been found out yet.

In practice, this looks like messing around on the internet. Consider: I have a research project right now with Damien Huffer that, while being about the trade of human remains on the internet, is also about the limits of computer vision for digital archaeology and digital history. I proposed this project not knowing anything about what a distant, corpus-scale view of photographic materials might achieve. I had some experience in macroscopic approaches to textual materials, so the approach to teach myself the potentials—to learn enough so that I could write the proposal—is the same.

First I read the hype. What are all the amazing whiz-bang things that people are doing or say that the tech can do? Then I look for all the caveats. Sometimes this takes a while because the whiz-bang stage for digital approaches can last a long time. Next, I start to write the tutorial that someday I'll give to my students: why should you care about x; what has x been used for; where might x be used in digital history/digital archaeology; what does x depend on to work. There's always a lot of blanks at first. Until you get it up and running, you have no idea how convolutional neural networks (for instance; a way of representing visual information as weighted networks through interconnecting layers of computational neurons) might be useful for archaeologists. Isn't it neat the way it can identify and caption a picture of a cat, though? I'll come back to this tutorial over and over again. Parts of it will first see the light of day as blog posts, as I figure out the sequence of commands for fiddly bits.

Most packages of interesting code will have a GitHub repository. I'll search GitHub for keywords that I've learned from reading the hype. At some point, I discovered that Macs come with Python installed by default. Anything written in Python, I'll prioritize exploring. As a result of all that exploration of textual materials, I've also learned a bit about R, so if things are written in R, well, I know how to run those, too.

Once I find some interesting packages, I start trying to make sense of their documentation. I don't waste my time on packages with poor documentation. If it seems reasonably clear, then the challenge of installing all of the supporting bits-and-pieces begin. I spend a lot of time on Stack Overflow, searching the names and phrases and general ideas, trying to work out which element is key, or if any will do, and if so, how to do it. On my blog, I document what I've done, where I've searched, what I've tried, the sequence of commands. Or at least, I try to. Sometimes I don't, and when I return to the problem in a week, two weeks, a month, I pretty much have to start over again.

I make some headway. I start to understand some of the more high-level, Granny Weatherwax-style posts. I get stuck. I search for Magrat-style posts, tweets, whatever I can find. If I find an actual tutorial, I try to work through it. I get stuck. The cycle starts again.

I try to update my own tutorial. I ask questions on Twitter, on my blog. I email people. Sometimes I know them, sometimes I get to know them. I vent on social media. I draw strength from others who can commiserate. I sit down at the terminal and invoke the magical words that will cause things to happen. Things crash, break. I copy the cryptic error messages, use them as the basis of a new search.

It might look like messing around on the internet, but there's a cycle of exploration, documentation, experimentation, consideration of results, documentation, exploration, documentation, experimentation . . . When it breaks: is it the tech that's broken? Is it me, something I don't understand, some kind of scaffolding I'm missing? Hey, it works—if I deliberately try to break it, when does it break? Where? Why? Under what conditions? Human remains are consistently identified by the neural network model provided by Google as "jellyfish." Why is that? What if we throw out the identifications, grab the next layer down: is this information useful? What can I do with it? Write it down. Blog it. Turn it into an article. Share.

Research witchcraft in action.

Horses to Water

The professor looked around the room brightly (or at least, as brightly as one can on a Monday morning in March). "So let's talk about your final projects. Where are we at? What's working, where can we troubleshoot?"

Murmurs from the class. Someone volunteered, "Going well, just have to meet later today to talk about it." Another said "Having trouble making variables work. Has anyone run into . . . ?" All good stuff.

The last group:

"Yep, we've got everything written out in a Word doc, which is in Dropbox."

"You're working on a code project . . ."

"Yes?"

". . . which involves collaborating on code . . ."

"Yes?"

". . . for which we've invested considerable time and energy in learning how to use a digital tool explicitly meant to facilitate asynchronous collaboration on code . . ."

"Yes?"

". . . code which carries all sorts of syntactical information in its use of spaces or tabs and special characters, and thus needs to be composed in an environment that does not add any hidden information . . ."

"Yes?"

". . . and you're writing it using Word?"

"We color coded each person's contributions so that you can see who wrote what and divvy up the grade appropriately."

Horses led to water do not necessarily always drink.

There are powerful currents in any class, a kind of self-organization that emerges from each student's trajectory through the program. The things that happen in the class itself, that is to say, the course work, can very often be the least critical things happening in a student's life. Students also have the challenges that they are facing in their private lives, the need to pay increasing tuition, the dropping levels of financial aid. The fail in the story above might appear at first blush to be that of the students: so fixated on grades that they miss the entire point of the work. The fail might be the professor's: the point of the work is not clear or meaningful enough. Perhaps the professor has failed to consider the game of being a student which, at my most cynical, means jumping through hoops to get the piece of paper to get a job. The professor is certainly not being kind, playing the experience for laughs out of frustration, mangling the old saying. Perhaps the fail here is the institution which, in its lack of trust, forces student work through plagiarism detection software and makes progress through the hoops contingent on particular grades. Things that break, that are experimental, that don't work, are too much risk. Play it safe.

Whatever's going on, it wouldn't take much to alter the trajectory towards a win:

". . . and you're writing it using Word?"

"We color coded each person's contributions so that you can see who wrote what and divvy up the grade appropriately."

"Interesting. How did you come to that decision? Why did you feel you needed to do that?"

Letter to a Young Scholar

I sometimes receive notes from undergrads or other folks wondering what advice I have about studying to become "X". Below is a response I wrote to a student who wanted to go to grad school with an eye toward pursuing a professorship in classical archaeology.

Hi _____ ,

Thank you for your note, and your query about how I got here and various options for your own path. I'll tell you first about my own journey. Don't let that part put you off, but I want you to have your eyes open as you consider your options.

My own personal journey is perhaps not a template to follow. I went to the UK for grad school in Roman archaeology. At the end of that process, I was teaching random courses at universities across the southeast of England, piecing together enough money to keep me going, living out of a rucksack. I eventually got tired of that and came back to Canada where I was, for all intents and purposes, unemployable in Canadian archaeology. I tried to start some businesses. I substitute taught at a local high school. I did whatever was necessary to make ends meet. Eventually I got a position working online for a for-profit "university" in the US, which gave me a bit of stability. Eventually, I saw the job advertisement for a position in digital humanities at Carleton, and here I am.

So my journey involved transforming myself from frankly a second-rate Roman epigraphist into a digital humanities scholar and digital archaeologist. I benefited from being in the right place at the right time, having made a bit of a name for myself by blogging my continuing research throughout that period. There was a lot of luck involved.

Between December 2002, when I received my PhD, and July 2010, when I started at Carleton, I had precisely two interviews for full-time academic postings.

Now, the keys to getting the job at Carleton were that when I returned to Canada, I had to work extremely hard to make connections with people in the community I wanted to be a part of. Conferences, open research online. Contract archaeology wanted nothing to do with me because I had not gained enough experience in field archaeology in the UK to be employable in Canada. Cultural heritage work is more the province of historians in this country.

My advice, for what it's worth:

- I'd have still gone to the UK for grad school, but I would not necessarily jump into doing a PhD. Few places in this world are better for archaeology, ancient civilizations, etc. An MA opens opportunities; a PhD can be perceived as narrowing your range of options—you have to work hard to convince people of the worth of the PhD, that it makes you better in the long run for a wide variety of things.
- Follow the money: go where they really want you. If a school offers some sort of scholarship, I'd take it. My first year of MA studies in the UK doubled my entire debt up to that point. Tuition fees for foreigners have only gotten worse in the UK. The cost may not be worth the pain.
- Do an MA that fills you with joy, as Marie Kondo would put it—it's one of the few times in this life where you can choose that. An MA of any stripe is all to the good, so don't fall into the instrumentalist trap of picking something that you think someone else (however construed) would approve of.

- A classical MA, of whatever stripe, can be a very good foundation for a wide variety of paths in this life. Don't worry necessarily about the job at the end of it. Classical folks, in my experience, tend to be some of the most creative and lateral thinking people I've ever met.
- Be aware that grad school *will* take a toll on your mental health. Make plans to keep your support networks, your friendships, intact. Have hobbies. It's ok to not work on weekends.
- I'd have focused on getting more fieldwork. That said, archaeology suffers from gendered labor issues such that it is largely men in positions of power. So if you plan on trying for an archaeological career in fieldwork, know that this is an issue.
- Classics departments are greying, but they are not necessarily hiring to replace retirements.
- Work constantly on your digital literacy: skills, trends, research methods, questions, theories.
- Develop a scholarly online presence.
- Lurk on Twitter, follow scholars whose work fills you with wonder or whom you admire. Follow a couple you loathe, for a contrary view.

You might also wish to frame your interests a bit more broadly and consider in what other contexts you can engage with Greek and Roman civilizations—museums, digital work, community, public, game studies, and so on.

Best wishes,
Shawn

I heard and responded to the question on the surface, and I left it at that. I did this student a disservice. Why was this student asking how to be a professor? That was the question I didn't ask. Not your problem, you might think. But it is. It certainly is.

Anne Helen Petersen put her finger on it: our students are burnt out from the need to be optimal. The rest of us have created a world that is always on, that sees every moment as optimized for some metric or other. Something from which value can be extracted. A world so precarious every waking moment has to be shaped towards the goal. People sneer at millennials and their "flaky ways," but Petersen is right: these are symptoms of burn out. She writes, of her current students:

> Every graduating senior is scared, to some degree, of the future, but this was on a different level. [...] these students were convinced that their first job out of college would not only determine their career trajectory, but also their intrinsic value for the rest of their lives. [...] students internalize the need to find employment that reflects well on their parents (steady, decently paying, recognizable as a "good job") that's also impressive to their peers (at a "cool" company) and fulfills what they've been told has been the end goal of all of this childhood optimization: doing work that you're passionate about. (2019)

And the end goal *isn't there*. The reward, the pot-of-gold at the end of this careful monitoring, tailoring, pushing, pruning—it's just not there. And if you do find it, the reward for doing work you're passionate about is just more work. And if you're passionate about it, why, you'd do it for less, right?

Because passion. The unsaid question of the student who wrote to me was really "I don't know what to do next. I'm only good at school. I'm passionate about education. What do I do?"

Why couldn't I see this? I was that student, once. I was good at school. I did everything I was supposed to do. I fell, once I got through to the other side. But I don't think I was ever as burnt out as I see so many students are today. Petersen goes on to say:

> I never thought the system was equitable. I knew it was winnable for only a small few. I just believed I could continue to optimize myself to become one of them. And it's taken me years to understand the true ramifications of that mindset. I'd worked hard in college, but as an old millennial, the expectations for labor were tempered. We liked to say we worked hard, played hard—and there were clear boundaries around each of those activities. Grad school, then, is where I learned to work like a millennial, which is to say, all the time. (2019)

The advice I gave has some good points, I suppose, although as I write this the world has gone mad and I'd be very leery of sending students to the UK in the confusion of Brexit. But my advice really just sets the student up to work harder, for longer, at greater financial, emotional, and mental cost: all the factors in the burnout that Petersen identifies. We have no business doing that to our students. Maybe what I could be doing is not offering advice, but putting my energy instead into designing my courses so that I don't create an environment that requires work (labor) all the time. Instead, I can concentrate on creating an environment that allows for experimentation, serendipity, collisions, and joy: glorious failures. Where it's ok to have the smartphone and the computer turned off. Where the learning management system isn't used to spy on the students. I can't fix this damned world and what it's become. But maybe I can carve out a corner where optimization is not required, where that burden can be put down for a while. Doesn't archaeology teach that context is everything? I could start by trying to understand that of my students.

Dear ____ ,

Thank you for your note. I'd like to chat with you; could I buy you a coffee? Perhaps we could pick apart why you want to be a professor and identify the things that are meaningful about that for you. There might be other paths that could move you closer to those things (which may or may not be found in academia). Becoming a professor is something that sadly involves an awful lot of luck and good timing as much as anything else (and perhaps more). I was lucky, after a very long time of being unlucky.

Best wishes,
Shawn

There's a difference between listening and telling.

I Don't Know How to Do This

I wrote this piece after becoming aware of the distress a former student was in. I too often try to fix things instead of listening. While I cared deeply, I could not find the words then. Later, I wrote this and posted it online in 2016.

I don't know how to do this.

I worry that whatever I did say would only make it worse. How do you help? Your students never stop being your students. You work with them for days on end, through periods of intense frustration, through times of amazing energy and excitement, to joy (graduation!) I've been teaching one way or another, on and off, since about 2003. Some of my students have gotten married, had kids, got great jobs. Some spin their wheels, idly, not knowing how to move forward. Some have taken their own lives or died in accidents. Some soldier on when all hell breaks loose around them, when their world is turned upside down through no fault of their own. You care about them all. But.

I don't know how to do this.

It's hard enough to handle the shit that happens to me. Or to see the path before my own kids and know what kinds of rocks and weeds and rakes-in-the-grass lie in wait. Then you add all these other people who have entrusted some part of their lives to you. Every day, your students are not just people to whom you perform. Your life is entangled with theirs. Granted, it's a weird kind of entanglement (that shock of recognition when they encounter you outside the appropriate setting), but it exists. It persists. They are always your students. But.

I don't know how to do this.

I don't know how to help. "We're not trained for this! We're not mental health professionals!" we say, when what we fear for is our own mental health. I write this tonight, having read the things my students write, and I think about how much easier it would be to just retreat into my shell, to switch off, to harden. I don't know how to do that either, and so I get overwhelmed.

I don't know how to do this.

You see people hurting, and you suspect that maybe, in this one small corner of the world, in this one little bit where all is contained and sorted and regulated and boxed in, in this thing that is your class, this is the one place where the right word could make the difference. Where it could keep things together for one more day. Where it won't necessarily fix things, but it'll certainly not make it worse. Where it would show a little bit of unexpected kindness. But.

There is no one thing I could say to make it better. Yet I marvel at these students' strength, their determination, and in that, I find that maybe I do know how to do this. I don't need to say anything; I just need to be.

To be present.

To be aware.

To be open.

I can do this.

The fail here is the failure to reach out and do the right thing. There is no glorious fail, in this case. This is an entirely different register. In earlier stories, my empathy or lack thereof prevented me from doing the thing that could provide the space my students needed. Here, my desire to do something is tempered by the knowledge that maybe I'm not the person to be doing it. Emotional labor is distributed unequally; maybe it was the wrong choice. Some days later, after posting, a colleague whom I did not know at a university in the US wrote to me. He reached out because he was struggling with supporting his students in distress. There were no resources at his institution to deal with the mental health issues that emerge when we open ourselves to the pain and the needs of our students. I looked at my own institution and saw a similar lack. He was writing to express relief that he was not the only one who felt similarly without a map and compass. The post made it OK for him to acknowledge his concern about his students, to make peace with not knowing what to do, for he was not alone. Doing right by others: sometimes a simple blog post will land where it's needed, not where you thought it was going.

Part Four

Possibilities

I still don't know what the digital humanities are. Or is it "is?" Data are, data is? I'm still learning, every day. Before I applied for the job in 2010, which required a specialist in the digital humanities, I had only once used the term on my blog. It simply wasn't on my radar. In this section, I recount a few key episodes in my journey toward the digital humanities and some of the things that I've learned along the way.

Your digital humanities will be different, of course.

What Is This Thing?

Where does the narrative of your fails go? How does failing gloriously become digital humanities? Purpose and paradata.

The student was at my door, nearly in tears. "I don't think my work is digital humanities, and I know I have to have 30% be digital humanities or else it doesn't count."

Or,

"I think something 'dh-y' would be good for my resume. What if I built an exhibit?"

Or,

"It'd be interesting to know how all of these people connect up, I've got these letters and I think this person knew everyone."

Or,

"Wouldn't it be neat if when you stood in front of a monument you started hearing competing voices telling *their* side of the story?"

Or,

"Can you teach me some statistics? I've got all this data but I don't know what it means."

Or,

"Why can't we just put in the requirements that a digital project is a website or podcast?"

As the official digital historian in the department, I field lots of interesting questions from students and colleagues as they work on their research. Some of them are motivated from an instrumentalist desire, a need to put skills on a CV or to tick off some administrative box. Our digital humanities program sits across several different departments, all with their own disciplinary traditions and views on what constitutes digital work or how much of a thesis must be "digital," however construed, in order to count. Our program committee meets periodically throughout the year to address these questions and figure out whether or not the work students do in the digital humanities program is sufficiently "dh-y" under the rubrics and quality assurance documents that the university and the province use. Is this digital humanities? How would we know?

To categorize something is to reveal what you think is important. Digital humanities is a moving target. It needs to be a few steps back of the latest computational wizardry emerging in other fields in order to figure out both what the technology can do for us and what the technology *does* to us. Mere technology use is therefore not a useful dimension to measure. Let me lay out what I think are two useful dimensions for creating typologies of digital humanities work.

The first extends along a continuum we could call purpose, from discovery through to justification. This framing comes from my reading of Trevor Owen's piece on "Science-ing the Humanities," on the differences between computational work to confirm or refute a hypothesis versus computational work that seeks to explore a problem space:

> When we separate out the context of discovery and exploration from the context of justification we end up clarifying the terms of our conversation. There is a huge difference between "Here is an interesting way of thinking about this" and "This evidence supports this claim." (2012)

The closer we get to discovery work, the more it might fit into the worldview of the digital humanities. Discovery necessarily involves trying many different things out, and trying things out is just another way of saying failure-as-epistemology. If we are using computational power to deform our texts, then we are trying to see things in a new light and new juxtapositions to spark new insight. Ramsay talks about this too in Reading Machines, discussing the work of Jerome McGann and Lisa Samuels: "Reading a poem backward is like viewing the face of a watch sideways—a way of unleashing the potentialities that altered perspectives may reveal." (33) Alternatively, there is a lot of computational work that seeks to explore, understand, and ground observations in the data, work that justifies a particular reading or supports it. One is not superior to the other. They are merely different and any project might have different admixtures of these two perspectives at any one time.

The other dimension concerns computing skill/knowledge and its explication. It's not the kinds of skills here I am thinking about, but rather how well we fill in the blanks for others. The documentation of our failure-as-epistemology. That is to say, how we talk about what we needed to learn in order to do the digital work. There is so much tacit knowledge in the digital world. Read any tutorial, and there's always some little bit that the author has left out, some little gotcha, because well, isn't that obvious? Do I really need to tell you that? I'm afraid the answer is yes. "Good" work is work that provides an abundance of detail about how the work was done so that a complete neophyte can replicate it. This doesn't mean that it has to be right there in the main body of the work—it could be in a detailed FAQ, a blog post, or a stand-alone site. But it does have to be accessible, it does have to be open, and it should be archived in a digital repository somewhere.

I once decided to start a project that used Neatline, the mapping plugin for Omeka. Having put together a couple of Omeka sites before, and having played around with adding plugins, I found that the documentation supporting Neatline is quite robust. Nevertheless, I became stumped on the problem of the GeoServer to serve up my georectified historical maps. Over the course of a few days, I discovered that since

GeoServer is java-based, most website hosting companies charge a premium or monthly charge to host it. Not only that, it needs Apache Tomcat installed on the server first, to act as a container. I eventually found a site—Openshift—that would host all of this for free (cost and sustainability is always an issue for the one-man-band digital humanist), but to use that service required me to install Ruby and Git on my machine, then to clone the repository to my own computer, then to drop a WAR file into the webapps folder (but there are two separate webapp folders), then "commit, push" everything back to OpenShift. Then I found some tutorials that were explicitly about putting GeoServer on OpenShift, so I followed them to the letter, but it turned out they were out of date.

The time involved in learning all of this was considerable, and at the end of the day, I still had nothing to show for it. (Incidentally, one of the people from OpenShift saw my tweets of frustration and tried to coach me through things, so chalk one up for open process!) What I did have was a much better understanding of how all of these different pieces of software interact to create the engagement with the archaeological data I wanted to map, and the decisions I had to make to achieve this. The hidden layer of digital plumbing changes the experience of the story I was trying to tell. The hidden layer has to be surfaced, in good digital humanities work.

An importance axis for evaluating work in the digital humanities is the quality of explication of process. The London Charter for the computer-based visualization of cultural heritage calls this paradata. Since so much of what we do consists of linking together lots of disparate parts, we need to spell out how all the different bits fit together and what the neophyte needs to do to replicate what we've just done.

"Purpose and Paradata," I said to the student. "Where does your work fall along purpose and paradata? Your work is digital humanities, it's just a kind we haven't seen yet."

Rehashing Archaeology

Asked to speak at a workshop on digital archaeology, reusing digital data, and teaching, I had to provide a title. "Rehashing Archaeology," I said, pulling it out of the air. This is the text of that talk, which I delivered in 2017 via video link because I declined to travel to the United States for conferences during the Trump travel bans. While this piece does not explicitly reference failing gloriously as I have developed it in this volume, compare what I describe as a rehashed archaeology with the pedagogy of failing gloriously and I think it will be clear how the philosophy informs what I am describing.

What is rehashing archaeology? Well, to rehash something (per the American Heritage Dictionary) is:

- Verb: To bring forth again in another form without significant alteration: *rehashing old ideas*.
- Verb: To discuss again.

Bit of a negative connotation there. I asked on Twitter, as you do, what people thought I meant by rehashing archaeology, as I hadn't figured it out yet. Titles first, thinking later, eh? The responses were helpful.

Stu Eve suggested: Saying the same thing that has been said before but in a slightly different way to avoid plagiarism?

Ted Underwood chimed in: Fossilized hash browns. Or possibly HashMaps.

Lorna Richardson asked: Is it rearranging what digital archaeology stands for/means, away from current understanding?

I like these. I want to discuss digital archaeology in all of these terms. Digital archaeology and digital data may as well not exist unless they get rehashed. The problem is, how do you teach this?

Let's start with Stu's idea, but reframe it in terms of citations. True confession time—I Google myself to see where my work is being cited. My numbers, insofar as Google Scholar is true, look fairly good. I can take this as indicative of a kind of reuse of my archaeological data, right? My studies are being cited, ergo the work I did is useful to someone else, ergo, it is being reused. But when you go deeper into this reuse, you find that it's surface-y. It's a bit disappointing, really, to think your career is filler for someone else's padding. Or, as Paul O'Donnel once put it, your entire life's work is just an academic "compulsory figure."

I have a topic model of 20,000 archaeological journal articles from the 1930s to the 2010s, and no topic within it uses the words "reuse," "reproducible," or "reanalyze" in any meaningful way. "Data" is prominent in two topics, but always in the context of new data. While we might revisit an issue from time to time, no one is analyzing someone else's data in any meaningful way in the broader noise of academia, per this topic model.

It would seems that nobody is rehashing archaeology, which is a sobering thought. Maybe part of the problem is packaging. We don't play nice with each other. In our heart of hearts, we don't want other people looking at our data. You see this in embryo when you try to force students to work together on a project. Reusing data is a group project where your group members live in the future, and you just know they're going to be angry with you.

And will the data they play with be the data you left behind? How will they know? In this era of assaults on rationality and truth, where the data you download has no guarantee that it's the same data that was uploaded, we have to be on guard for deliberate alterations.

This leads me to make a tie-in to Ted's comment about HashMaps. A hash function takes any input and maps it to a particular value. It's deterministic. If the input changes—say a text file gets edited and something gets deleted—the hash at the other end is changed.

There are many useful things one can do with this information. In security, it can be used to test that a message hasn't been changed en route. Or, it can be used to search a database only for things that have changed. Knowing that our data has not been corrupted is becoming ever more important. We need to become familiar with hash functions in order to guard against malicious uses of archaeology for political ends.

There are other uses for hash functions in archaeology, of course. In my own work with Damien Huffer on the trade in human remains facilitated via social media, we've been using Lincoln Mullen's R package for detecting text reuse via hash functions to trace patterns in this trade. It turns out that text reuse is a very useful signature for individual buyers' and sellers' writing patterns (thanks to auto-correct and adaptive/predictive text on our phones and keyboards), even when there's no ID otherwise associated with the post. Be sure your sins will find you out.

But again, how do you teach archaeology students these things? It doesn't look like archaeology. Which leads me to Lorna Richardson's comment on digital archaeology perhaps being a pivot away from how we've done things in the past to how we might do things in the future.

Lorna's research is extremely important for digital archaeology. One of the things she focuses on is what might be called the consumption side of archaeology within the web—of what is lately known as fake news but was formerly called propaganda. We want people to engage with archaeology, right? If people reuse archaeology, how do we teach them to do it correctly and in good faith? Lorna's work looks at what's happening on Neo-Nazi websites and their rehashing of archaeology and archaeological data for white supremacist ends. How do we counter this? Are our current approaches to teaching archaeology effective for the wider impact of archaeological knowledge in society?

I understand digital archaeology as necessarily a public archaeology, and I think that means that all three aspects of this rehashing have to be part of that. Let me share some things I'm trying, some which seem to be working and some that have not.

Eric Kansa and I hatched a scheme to promote reuse of archaeological data published via OpenContext. "We'll provide incentives!" we thought. We offered real money, up to $1,000 in prizes, for teams or individuals to make the best visualization of the data using open-source software. We set up a panel of experts to judge the entries. We promoted the contest in every venue we could think of. We made videos, we wrote tutorials, we contacted professors across the world to encourage student participation.

Cue the tumbleweeds, for we had very little uptake.

Money is not enough it seems. But I wonder if part of the problem is that we're dealing with a sunk cost effect. So much of our computational archaeological infrastructure is proprietary software and databases for which we've paid licensing fees. We've paid so much money, we better damn well make sure that there is someone in our department or company who can use ArcGIS. Because this department, this company, uses ArcGIS, it makes sense to teach that. But all this open source stuff? All these new formats? Who uses it? It's a classic chicken-and-egg problem.

Two other problems: one, there is little culture of undergraduate teaching with actual datasets ready to take advantage of the opportunity. Two, working with digital data still requires a level of digital literacy that we haven't yet reached in the field.

These are manifestations of some other, more basic problems that confront us when we try to teach these tools, approaches, and perspectives.

Firstly, there is tremendous anxiety about digital technologies. My students, if I can coax them through the door, are not in any way naturally conversant with this. "If I wanted to do computers, I wouldn't have taken history," said a student in one of my courses. "What if it breaks? What if it doesn't work? How do I get an A?"

Secondly, the fear of failure curtails ambition. We have not taught students how to fail productively. We have created systems where the risks of trying something different are usually catastrophic. Digital work requires the "screwmeneutical imperative," as Stephen Ramsay famously put it (2014). Screwing around should appear on the learning objectives portion of the syllabus, but it never does.

Thirdly, the learning materials that are freely available often forget to surface the tacit knowledge required to make things work. Tech changes too rapidly, and the kinds of machines that students are sold are not necessarily the kind that can be usefully employed in this work. I've had students turn up to my dataviz digital humanities course with nothing more than an iPad mini. I also end up spending two or three weeks getting everyone's machines properly configured.

My mom thinks I primarily do tech support. She's mostly right.

So what can we do about this? How about we turn our teaching inside out. We do it in public. I'm not talking about 'massively open online courses', or MOOCs, though I suppose they have a role here, as educational tourism. No, I mean we literally put all of our teaching out there and invite the public to take part alongside our formal students. We share what has worked for us and what hasn't with our students and the public. We publish studies where the hypothesis didn't work out.

We replicate, again with our students and the public, someone else's study.

This will be dangerous, doing work in public. You're a white male on the internet? Put that to use. Get out there and take risks, and make it safe for others to do so, too.

It will require special tools. I'm building one right now with Neha Gupta, Michael Carter, and Beth Compton called the Open Digital Archaeology Textbook Environment (ODATE, http://o-date.github.io), which is a series of lessons, reflections, and self-contained computational environments that can run on any machine with a single click. With ODATE, we're trying to shift the infrastructure cost of learning to do digital archaeology from the student, from the individual, to us. Build once, deploy everywhere, as they used to say. To do digital archaeology should require only a browser. Taking our cue from OpenContext, we include recipes for different kinds of tasks alongside the more formal learning activities.

Digital archaeology is an opportunity to rethink how we do things and put a positive hash on rehashing the past. This is what rehashing digital archaeology really means. We have to enable people to reuse our data for themselves. That way, the possibility will at least exist that they can see the truth of what is being argued. But rehashing is going to take a lot of work.

Small Acts of Disruption

Failing gloriously means making space for others to fail productively, to use one's privilege and position to help others get ahead. As agent-based modeling and complexity theory teaches, simple rules can lead to complex behavior and small causes can lead to big effects. Fail gloriously is one such simple rule, no? At the Computer Applications in Archaeology 2018 conference, I spoke on this theme in the context of the disruptive digital archaeology session, exploring some small acts of disruption in archaeological publishing, using my position to make space for others to experiment.

What are some small acts of disruption that we can do in archaeological publishing, and why might they matter? Why should we be disruptive? The first small thing is to realize that ethical considerations have to be front and center with digital archaeology, that we have to begin from an ethical perspective. Allison Parish, a poet and programmer at NYU, once said, "A computer program is a way of projecting power. That's the point of a computer program, to make a decision and then have it happen millions of times. That's the real ethical dimension of this for me" (2018).

A computer program is a way of projecting power. Whose power? Onto whom? How? Why? The decisions taken in a digital medium, given the nature of computation (whose fundamental action is to copy), get multiplied in their effects. Hence, the choices, when there is a choice to be made (as there always is), are a force multiplier for what we think is important. That is why digital archaeology ought to begin with ethics.

Start from these first principles:

- Fundamental action of the computer: to copy
- Fundamental result of copying: connection
- Fundamental consequence of connection: extended sensorium
- Digital archaeology is an extended kind of digital kinaesthetia

Miguel Sicart writes on the ethics of video games, drawing on the work of Luciano Floridi, a philosopher of information. In his framework, Floridi treats everything that exists as informational objects or processes, including biological and other entities, all the way into databases and software agents. In a nutshell, everything that exists does so in relation to everything else, with at least some minimum worth. Thus anything that destroys or diminishes data is entropy or morally evil. Expanding on Floridi, Sicart writes:

> Information ethics describes a moral universe [an infosphere] in which not only is no being alone, but every being is indeed morally related to other beings, because in their well-being is connected the welfare of the whole system. [Journals] are systems that affect larger systems with their actions, affecting themselves as well, since other systems are procedurally and informationally related to them. [. . .] Information ethics considers moral actions an information process. (130)

He said "Agents"; I swapped in "Journals" as agents that disseminate archaeological information.

In the case of journals, consider the paywall. To erect a paywall is an immoral act because it promotes entropy, it diminishes informational entities. There's a difference between buying a copy of a magazine at a reasonable price and an academic paywall that is designed to force the purchase of subscription bundles at usurious rates. A paywall barrier is a form of power. This is why open access is so dangerous and so readily attacked or mischaracterized. The apparatus of academic journals, as we know and love them today, concentrated in the hands of a few super-publishers, fundamentally prevent connection, knowing-at-a-distance.

Connection is a kind of sensation. What gets sensed, what is permitted to be sensed and by whom, when and how such sensations are appropriated, the consensus around such things—the work of Yannis Hamilakis points to how these questions of aesthetics are ontologically similar to questions for politics (415). The work of Sara Perry on enchantment points to how we (as archaeologists) have excised wonder and affective engagement from our work by framing archaeology within a crisis model. A model built around enchantment opens us to connection again; to fight information entropy, we need to restore sensation, that digital archaeological kinaesthesia of distant knowing. In thinking through what an affective sensorality or enchanted approach could do for our work in a digital sphere, we might have some small responses to the ethical challenges foregrounded by Parrish and Sicart.

Here are two things that I am doing, two small disruptions that speak to these challenges. Feel free to tell me that I'm wrong.

The first is a born-digital journal for creative engagement in history and archaeology that I established called *Epoiesen*, which has at its core a focus on the affectivity of digital or other creative work. Epoiesen means "made" and implies a sensory engagement with the past. The term also appears on Greek pottery, a claim and boast of the artist's skills. This pottery was largely for export and so traveled about, a kind of ceramic social network diffusing the latest innovations.

One small act, which also ties to video game ethics: one might argue that games, as a native art form of the digital age, are only ethical if the choices within are meaningful or consequential. In which case, digital platforms have to embody meaningful choices for the agency of the human. Thus publishing in *Epoiesen* also has to give the author a meaningful choice. The authors published in *Epoiesen* can choose the terms under which their work is published. The authors can also choose the format, whether that is text, photos, art, interactives, or some other format yet to be devised. Collaborative reading and annotation is built in using the hypothes.is annotation service (an act of connectivity between authors and readers).

Another small act: *Epoiesen* attempts to future proof the digital work by requiring text, data, or code be written in simple formats, an act of information ethics to maintain the integrity of the informational entity.

Another small act: *Epoiesen* is about reframing peer review. Here, peer review (a relatively novel development in the humanities tout court, by the way) is not about quality assurance, nor about guarding the borders, nor is it anonymous. Instead, it is about creating new webs of relationships and new conservations. Instead of reviewers, I seek out respondents who write their own responses to the work, which are then published alongside it. With *Epoiesen*, I see publishing as a starting point, not a finish line. Responses, like the main pieces, are published with digital object identifiers to recognize the value of the labor and allow the response to enter the citation ecosystem.

The second small disruption is the Open Digital Archaeology Textbook Environment (ODATE). ODATE is a digital archaeology textbook environment that sits in the same sensory framework as *Epoiesen*. It comes with pre-loaded computational notebooks. Digital archaeology—to learn it, to challenge it, to dispel the magic of Apple's training us to expect "it just works"—needs us to open the hood. To learn digital archaeology well, there can be no disembodied distance from the work of the machine. Hamilakis has argued that archaeology is a device of modernity that relies on a sense of autonomous and disembodied vision; yet at the same time, to do archaeology means we have to be embodied in the moment, engaged with the things and environment. The digital world could be seen as similarly autonomous and disembodied—after all, there is a computer in the way—and thus digital archaeology somehow makes for a lesser archaeology, a more distant archaeology, a fast archaeology. Speaking for myself (though I suspect it is true of anyone who has tried to get their computer to do anything other than what Apple or Microsoft or Google permits or wants us to do), there is a sense of flow that comes from working with data and computation that is every bit as sensory and embodied as "dirt" archaeology.

Learning to use the machine in this way depends on slowly navigating a world built on organic metaphor, of streams and river branches and forks. Of growth and decay. Of ecologies and environments and webs of interdependencies. ODATE teaches digital archaeology within this framework, in particular, the Git ecosystem and GitHub code sharing platform. As an organic thing that grows and responds to our choices, it is always going to be wrong and out of date and close to failing. *That is a strength.* In this ecosystem, life depends on replicability, reproducibility, and the cutting and pasting of the bits that work for you. It will grow and there will be multiple copies—there will never be one canonical version of ODATE. That's a helluva disruption, right there.

To wind this up—small acts of disruption in archaeological publishing are actually large acts of disruption in how we think about, with, and through digital archaeology. If we think of archaeological publishing in terms of information ethics and archaeological senses, I think there's one final small act of disruption that flows from that, and it's this: we all can do this, already.

Some Assembly Required

I was asked to give a keynote on what digital humanities might do/ be for education to the Canadian Network for Innovation in Education in 2013. In this talk, the themes of failing gloriously, while still not fully fleshed out, can be seen to underpin this vision. After the piece there is a consideration of how well this 2013 vision of DH has held up. I include this piece here because at the end, it opens up a discussion about whether or not, or to what degree, failing gloriously should contain a public dimension. This brings us back full circle to the work of Katherine Cook.

I never appreciated how scary those three words were until I had kids: Some assembly required. That first Christmas was full of it. Slide Tab A into Slot B. Where's the 3/8ths gripley? Is that an Allen wrench? Why are there so many screws left over? The toys, with time, get broken, get fixed, get recombined with different play sets, are the main characters and the exotic locales for epic stories. I get a lot of mileage out of the stories my kids tell and act out with these toys.

Digital humanities, as I see it, is a bit like the way my kids play with the imperfectly built things—it's about making things, about breaking things, about being playful with those things. This talk is about what that kind of perspective might imply for our teaching and learning.

I don't know what persuaded my parents that it'd be a good idea to spend $300 in 1983 dollars on a Vic-20, but I'm glad they did. You turn on your iPad and it all just happens magically, whoosh! In those days, if you had a computer, you had to figure out how to make it do stuff the hard way. That first "Ready" prompt is a bit disappointing. Ready to do what? My brothers and I wanted to play games. So, we sat down to learn how to program them. My older brother got to run the keyboard, I got to read out the lines of code from the magazine, and my younger brother was in charge of snacks. 10 Print Chr$(205.5+Rnd(1)); : Goto 10. Go ahead. Find an emulator. Type that program in. If you had a Vic-20, do you remember how exciting it was when that maze first filled the screen? A bit like the apes in the opening scene of *2001: A Space Odyssey*. At least, in our house.

Wargame, the film with Matthew Broderick, came out around about the same time. This scared me, but I loved the idea of being able to reach out to someone else, someone far from where I lived in Western Quebec. Computers were *magical*. Powerful! So we settled for occasional trips to the Commodore store in Ottawa, bootleg copies of *Compute!* magazine, and my most treasured book, a how to make adventure games manual for kids, that my Aunt purchased for me at the Ontario Science Centre. Magic. Do you remember old-school text adventures? They're games! They promote reading! Literacy! They are a Good Thing. There was a lot of pedagogical energy expended in schools in those days on computers.

To play an interactive fiction is to foreground how the rules work; it's easy to see with interactive fiction. But that same interrogation needs to happen whenever we encounter digital media. When you play any kind of game or interact with any kind of medium, you generally achieve success once you begin to think like the machine. What do games teach us? How to play the game and how to think like a computer. This is a cyborg consciousness. The 'cyb' in cyborg comes from the Greek for governor or ship's captain. Who is doing the governing? The code. This is why humanities needs to consider the digital. It's too important to leave it to the folks who are already good at thinking like machines. This is the first strand of what digital humanities might mean.

A second strand comes from that same impulse that my brothers and I had—let's make something! Trying to make something on the computer inevitably leads to deformation.

This deformation can be on purpose, like an artist, or it can be accidental, a result of either the user's skill or the way that the underlying code imagines the world to work. One of the first pieces of code that I attempted to build myself was a toy called "Historical Friction." It was my attempt to realize a daydream: what if the history of a place was thick enough to impede movement through it?

I knew that I could find a) enough information about virtually everywhere on Wikipedia, that b) I could access this through mobile computing, and c) something that often stops me in my tracks is noise. But I don't have the coding chops to build something like that from scratch. What I can do, though, is mash things together. But when I do that, I'm beholden to design choices others have made. "Historical Friction" welded Ed Summer's *ici*, a tool for visualizing the geographical locations of Wikipedia articles within 500 meters of someone's location, with a voice synthesizer. Serendipitous connection with Stu Eve via Twitter meant that the toy became a joint effort and got us over the hard part of making the two things mesh. When it worked (which it did until Google changed too many of the security settings in Chrome), a chorus of digitized voices would read the Wikipedia articles, a cacophony so loud you'd have to turn it off and see the world with new eyes, reveling in the new silence.

This second strand of digital humanities is the deformance (with its connotations of a kind of performance) of different ways of knowing, and the insight that comes from reflection on the broken deformed things.

A third strand of digital humanities comes from the reflexive use of technology. My training is in archaeology. As an archaeologist, I became Eastern Canada's only expert in Roman brick stamps. Not a lot of call for that.

But I recognized that I could use this material to extract fossilized social networks, that the information in the stamps was all about connections. Once I had this social network, I began to wonder how I could reanimate it, and so I turned to simulation modeling. After much exploration, I've realized that what I give life to on these social networks is not the past, but rather the story I am telling about the past. I simulate historiography. I create a population of Roman golems (individual creatures, given life by the code/words in their head if you will) and I give them rules of behavior that describe some phenomenon in the past that I am interested in. These rules are formulated at the level of the individual. I let the golems go and watch how they interact. In this, I develop a way to interrogate the unintended or emergent consequences of the story I tell about the past: a kind of probabilistic historiography.

So digital humanities allows me to deform my own understandings of the world; it allows me to put the stories I tell to the test.

There's an awful lot of work that goes under the rubric of digital humanities. But these three strands are, I think, the critical ones for understanding what university teaching informed by digital humanities might look like. So let's consider then what digital humanities implies for university teaching.

But I feel I should warn you. My abilities to forecast the future are entirely suspect. As an undergrad in 1994, I was asked to go on this new thing called World Wide Web and create an annotated bibliography with as many websites as I could that dealt with the Etruscans. The first site I found (before the days of content filters) was headlined "The Sex Communist Manifesto." Unimpressed, I wrote a screed that began, "The so-called 'World Wide Web' will never be useful for academics."

My ability to forecast is suspect, at best.

Let me tell you about some of the things I have tried, built on these ideas of recognizing our increasingly cyborg consciousness, deformation of our materials, and of our perspectives. I'm pretty much a one-man band, so I've not done much with a lot of bells and whistles, but I have tried to foster a kind of playfulness, whether that's role-playing, game playing, or just screwing around.

Some of this has failed horribly, and partly the failure emerged because I didn't understand that, just like digital media, our institutions have rule sets that students are aware of. Sometimes, our best students are best not because they have a deep understanding of the materials, but rather because they have learned to play the games that our rules have created. In the game of being a student, the rules are well understood—especially in history. Write an essay; follow certain rhetorical devices; write a midterm; write a final. Rinse. Repeat. Woe betide the professor who messes with that formula!

I once taught in a distance ed program, teaching an introduction to Roman culture class. The materials were already developed; I was little more than a glorified scantron machine. I was getting essay after essay that contained clangers along the lines of, "Vespasian won the civil war of AD 69, because Vespasian was later the Emperor." I played a lot of Civilization IV at the time, so I thought, I bet if I could get students to play out the scenario of AD 69, The Year of the Four Emperors, students would understand a lot more of the contingency of the period, that Vespasian's win was not foreordained. I crafted the scenario, built an alternative essay prompt around it (play the scenario, contrast the game's history with real history), found students who had the game. Though many played it, they all opted to just write the original essay prompt. My failure was two-fold. One, playing a game for credit did not mesh with the game of being a student; there was no space there. Two, I created a "creepy treehouse," a transgression into the students' world where I did not belong. Professors do not play games. It'd be like inviting all my students to friend me on Facebook. It was weird.

I tried again, in a history course last winter. The first assessment exercise—an icebreaker, really—was to play an interactive fiction that recreated some of the social aspects of moving through Roman space. The player had to find their way from Beneventum to Pompeii without recourse to maps. What panic! What chaos! I lost a third of the class that week. Again, the concern was around how playing a game fit into the game of being a student. I assigned the playing of the game as a formal assessment piece—play the game, write a reflection on how this experience intersects with the academic readings on the spatial economy of the Roman world. "I know how to get an A with a paper. I don't know how to get an A here. How do I get an A?" Learning from the previous fiasco, I thought I'd laid a better foundation this time. Nope. The thing I neglected to notice was that there is safety in the herd. No one was willing to play as an individual and submit an individual response. "Who wants to be a guinea pig?" might have been the name of this game, as far as the students were concerned. I changed direction, and we played it as a group in class. Suddenly, it was safe.

But from failure we learn, and we sometimes have epic wins. Imagine if we had a system that short-circuited the game of being a student, that allowed students the freedom to fail, to try things out, and to grow! One of the major fails of my Year of the Four Emperors experiment was that it was I who did all the building. It should've been the students. When I built my scenario, I was doing it in public on one of the game's community forums. I've since started crafting courses (or at least, trying to) in which the students are continually building upward from zero in public, and all of their writing and crafting is done in the open, within the context of a special group. This changes the game considerably.

To many of you, this is no doubt a preaching-to-the-choir kind of moment. And again, I hear you say, what would an entire university look like, if all this was our foundation? Digital humanities will save us! It'll make the humanities relevant: to funding bodies, to government, to parents! Just sprinkle digital humanities fairy dust and all will be safe, right?

Sure. No doubt—a lot of folks are sick of hearing about the digital humanities. At the 2013 MLA convention, there was a good deal of pushback, including a session called "The Dark Side of Digital Humanities." Wendy Chun wrote:

> For today, I want to propose that the dark side of the digital humanities is its bright side, its alleged promise: its alleged promise to save the humanities by making them and their graduates relevant, by giving their graduates technical skills that will allow them to thrive in a difficult and precarious job market. Speaking partly as a former engineer, this promise strikes me as bull: knowing GIS or basic statistics or basic scripting (or even server side scripting) is not going to make English majors competitive with engineers or CS geeks trained here or increasingly abroad. [. . .] It allows us to believe that the problem facing our students and our profession is a lack of technical savvy rather than an economic system that undermines the future of our students.

She's right, of course. So how do we resist this instrumentalist impulse which erodes our teaching and learning? Following my three strands, we'd:

1. Identify the ways our institutions and our uses of technology force particular ways of thinking.
2. Deform the content we teach.
3. Set up our institutions and our uses of technology to deform the way our students think, including the ways our institutions are set up.

So let's turn the university inside out. We talk about knowledge being siloed, but I grew up on a farm: do you know what gets put into a silo, what comes out? It's silage, chopped up, often a bit fermented, cattle food, pre-processed cud. Let's not do that anymore. Whatever metaphor we use to frame what the university does, it goes a long way to framing the ways learning can happen. That's what digital humanities and its exploration of a cyborg consciousness should make us at least explore. And once we've done that, let's have some real openness. Let the world see the faculty-student and student-student relationships develop. Invite the rest of the world in.

Give every student, at the time of registration, a domain of their own, like the University of Mary Washington is starting to do. Pay for it, help the student maintain it during their time at university. At graduation, the student could either archive it or take over its maintenance. Let the learning community continue after formal assessment ends. The robots that construct our knowledge from the World Wide Web—Google and the content aggregators—depend on strong signals, on a creative class. If each and every student at your institution (and your alumni) is using a domain of their own as a repository for their own IP, a node in a frequently reconfiguring network of learners, your university would generate real gravity on the web.

Use the structure and logic of the web to embed the learning life of the university so deeply into the wider world that it cannot be extricated!

Right now, that's not happening. If you study the structure of the web for different kinds of academic knowledge, there's a huge disconnect between where the non-academics and the academics are. If we allow that to continue, it becomes increasingly easy for outsiders to frame academic knowledge as a synonym for pointless. With the embedded university, there are no outsiders. If we embed our teaching through the personal learning environments of our students, our research production will become similarly embedded. So what's tuition for, then? Well, it's an opportunity to have my one-on-one undivided attention; it's ice time, an opportunity to skate. But we need to have more opportunities for sideways access to that attention as well, to allow people who have benefited from participating in our openness to demonstrate what they've learned.

The digital humanities, as a perspective, has changed the way I've come to teach. I didn't set out to be a digital humanist; I wanted to be an archaeologist. But the multiple ways in which archaeological knowledge is constructed, its pan-disciplinary need to draw from different wells, pushed me into digital humanities. There are many different strands to digital humanities work, and I've identified here what I think are three major ones that could become the framework, the weave and the weft, for something truly disruptive.

2013 seems so long ago. To pick on one aspect of "some assembly required" that might not have held up very well: to talk about the university inside out feels woefully naive. It was a gesture toward recognizing the messy and complex processes through which we come to know something of the world, the antithesis to the easy analyses preferred by pundits and politicians. I was assuming a world of good-faith actors; as I said, woefully naive. In 2019, turning the university inside out would only expose the most precarious among us to further attack, and the impulses that I was trying to celebrate would be weaponized against anyone who tried it. Katherine Cook (2019) reminds us:

> The stubbornly DIY mentality that has come to characterize digital archaeology powered by and for inclusion and diversity emerged out of structures of inclusion and inequity but addressing the true crisis of scholarship endangering scholars today must be a Do-It-Collectively priority. (440)

Failing gloriously is a collective endeavor because it depends on imagining how things could be different. To do that requires engaging with people who do not look like you, who do not come from the same places or traditions as you do. By talking of the university inside out in 2013, I think I was perhaps grasping toward the idea of difference that opening things up would encounter. Failing gloriously is an exhortation to build spaces that make it safe for others to have the same freedom to make mistakes, tinker, iterate, and imagine better. *Epoiesen*, as a platform to recognize, valorize, and celebrate work that discusses its flaws and potentials is in fact the clearest distillation I think of failing gloriously that I can currently do. In 2019, we have to recognize that making it safe for others to fail is to be a builder of systems and a runner of interference. This can mean, as Cook points out, that sometimes we will have to block or disconnect in order to protect and shelter. *Epoiesen* has an annotation layer built on top of it, and perhaps, if it becomes abused, I will remove it. A humane digital humanities does not have to participate in the logics of ad-driven tech outrage.

Conclusion: To Walk in the Air

Some families go on long car trips to Disney World. I made my family, my parents and brothers, go on a road trip to a Classics conference. The Griswolds Do Session 17 On Roman Wall Styles. In 2003, I was convinced that *this is it*! This is the paper that will make my name! The paper that will thrust me into the limelight!

While the rest of my family had the good sense to go see what sights there were, I snuck my older brother into the conference. We passed a crowded meeting room where a "new" Greek vase was being revealed to the world (it had just turned up on the art market). We found the ballroom—"Look man, Ballroom Seven! It's huge! There'll be so many people here!"—and stepped inside.

Our footsteps echoed in the vastness.

Four individuals at the front.

One person in the audience—my brother.

He looked at me, raising an eyebrow as if to say, "We drove twelve hours for this?"

I read my paper to the other three presenters. The chair said, "Well, that was a modern approach."

And I was done.

It's not uncommon to see folks on Twitter tallying up the costs (financial and otherwise) of attending the major conferences, especially the ones that hold hiring interviews. I am glad I never got the call to go to any of those conference interview sessions; the practice is appalling. Nevertheless, I went to my fair share of conferences, spoke to my fair share of largely empty rooms, let my spirits hope that *this* time would be the one. How insulated I was, complaining about being ignored.

Of being a nobody. Far worse things can happen at conferences. And yet, for all I want to rail against conferences, I cannot deny that once—maybe not this time, but nevertheless, *once*—it worked and I made the vital connection.

If. If. If.

The sheer luck involved boggles the mind. On the other hand, it wasn't a lightning strike, you've-won-the-lottery kind of luck. At the time, I couldn't even tell that something lucky had happened. The future is only visible in retrospect.

We are trained to ignore and hide our luckiness, to pretend that luck wasn't there. To make a fetish of not-luck. Luck makes imposters of us all. If it's not luck, then the only answer is that it's your own damned fault, right? Your lack of a job/position/grant is a moral reflection on you, right? Another word for the institutionalized luck of those who have a lot already is "privilege." When we as a field or a department or a university take actions to make the possibility of luck more equitable for a broader swathe of people, that's when "this place is a meritocracy!" rears its head (a word coined to mock the very idea it is now taken to mean).

Not acknowledging the operations of luck makes us all sick. To feel like an imposter is to be aware of, and ashamed of, the role that luck has played. Don't be ashamed. Recognize the element of luck. Use the space that luck has afforded you to make space for others.

Fail gloriously.

In 2002 I graduated, proud and excited. I stepped out, into the air, and fell.

It hurts to fall flat on your face. Grad school and academia do a lot of damage. As we are damaged, so we damage others in turn. It can take some time to recover. I promised, in the opening, that there was a connective thread that tied all of these anecdotes and reflections together. The story of this book has been about what I learned after grad school, as I tried to pick myself back up. It's also a story of this moment though, where I am firmly entrenched in all of the systems that caused me so much damage in the first place.

Can you change things from the inside? I don't know. I can try so that other folks don't have to take a walk in the air like I did.

I tell myself over and over: Be kind. Don't be a jerk. Be human. Fail gloriously. Small changes can have large effects. Be present. Make space for others. Use your own position to build others up.

It's not about you anymore.

My experience is no guide for anyone else. But maybe, just maybe, it will make space for you to try something else.

My name is Shawn Graham, and I'm proud to be an imposter.

Afterword
Neha Gupta

... we don't have to do things the way we've been told they've always been done.

No one sets out to fail. And yet fails happen—they happen all the time, to each and every one of us. Fail is so ubiquitous that Silicon Valley technocrats have made it a mantra, reciting that champions (companies) are made from fails, from getting up after falling (bankruptcy) and learning as you go. With this ethos, the tech industry maintains its youthful spirit of exploration, experimentation, and life-long learning. What tech gurus grossly underestimate is privilege. The privilege of being a man, of European-heritage with social and professional networks and sufficient financial support to take those risks. Failure in public is a privilege that not everyone has because not everyone is a white man.

In *Failing Gloriously*, Shawn Graham describes himself as "a white tenured professor," "a white guy on the Internet," "an imposter," and a "storyteller" who learned to fail *productively*. He shares with us his personal journey of triumphs and failures to becoming a member of the professoriate. A reader unfamiliar with Shawn and his scholarship might see this volume as yet another publication on the Silicon Valley virtue of failing, invariably written by a white guy. One could distill and dismiss the volume in this way, but I would challenge the skeptic to keep reading. This is the book that technocrats didn't write because they didn't think it important to say how things could be different, how they are in positions to make space for productive learning or rather, how it could be safe for others to fail. As Shawn explains, "[to] fail gloriously is to use the privileges that you have, as you are able, to make it safe for others to fail."

A salient theme in Shawn's autobiography is the job crisis in academia and the fact that many doctoral graduates in archaeology, particularly in Canada, the United States, and the United Kingdom, do not secure permanent academic positions. This is not particular to archaeology, but rather it is a broader social phenomena that has been going on for decades. The number of faculty positions in departments have been reduced while the number of doctorates graduating has either remained constant or increased. Retiring professors are replaced not with similar permanent positions, but with contingent, term-to-term (adjunct/sessional) lectureships. In short, a scholar with an advanced degree is not guaranteed an academic position. This is the broader context of Shawn's narrative.

Scholars who are in graduate school, or those who have recently graduated and are struggling to land their first academic positions, however precarious, will read this volume differently. As a scholar who has been recently hired into the much coveted tenure-track position, I no longer have that precarity, and I am too close, too new to the professorate to reflect on where I have landed. I can say that the uncertainty of "what next" seamlessly makes way for "why was I hired," and "what did I do differently that I hadn't done before, years ago?" Now that I am on the other side of the table, how do I do differently? What can I do now so my students don't go blindly through their challenges? That is my journey.

Shawn's narrative is deeply personal; he leads us through the shock, disappointment, and embarrassment of not getting an academic position in the discipline that he trained for, reinventing himself and his research interests, teaching high school students and online courses, and then in 2010, securing an academic position in digital humanities. It is precisely in retelling his journey as one in which things didn't work out as he had imagined or hoped that glorious failing comes to life. *Acknowledge when something has not worked out.* Shawn generously shares with us details from some of his most difficult, humbling lessons, all of which have come from teaching university and high school students. *Be human*, he tells us. *Take the time to listen.*

Shawn frames the volume through Croxall and Warnick's (2015) schema for fails and Dombrowski's (2019) taxonomy of fails, which include technology fails, human fails, career planning and communication fails, and failures to probe assumptions and to do right by others. The last is at the heart of glorious failure. *Do the work that sets other people up for success.* Shawn tells us about his family: his Gramma's labor in bringing out the best in him, his father's work in building community, and his brother attending every wake and connecting with his community. In so doing, Shawn is gently urging the reader to consider what "work" and "building community" means in academia, encouraging us to think about what academia is and more importantly, to imagine how it could be different.

Digital humanities and digital archaeology are relatively young disciplinary specializations, even if their respective practitioners have long utilized computing tools and technologies. Shawn details his experiments with digital things, how they broke, and how he learned what went wrong. This is one facet of being the digital guy. Another facet is reporting back on what worked and what didn't. Shawn has maintained a blog of his experiments since 2006 at electricarchaeology.ca. There you will find a treasure trove of Shawn's projects, presentations, and how-to documentation of his experiments. He writes on what he tried, which bit of code worked, what failed and why. Find one and try it. Make it better. Report back.

That's how things move forward. It might seem easy to do this, but talk with anyone who has maintained a blog and ask what it takes to put your work out into the world. But that's why Shawn generously shares—to encourage others to do the same, to create the space where others can succeed.

Failing Gloriously is not a manual or a how-to. Read in one way, it reflects the rapidly changing higher education environment, giving insight into the life of an academic archaeologist in the final years of the twentieth century and the early twenty-first century as well as documenting the emergence and growth of digitally mediated scholarship in the social science and humanities. But Shawn achieves something profound and nuanced through the volume; he gives us all room to imagine a more humane academia, a more connected, collaborative community, and he offers a way toward that vision.

References

"Episode 46: Allison Parrish." *Commonplace: Conversations with Poets (and Other People)*, 14 Feb., https://www.commonpodcast.com/home/2018/2/14/episode-46-allison-parrish. 2018

Chun, Wendy. "The Dark Side of the Digital Humanities–Part 1" *Thinking C21* https://www.c21uwm.com/2013/01/09/the-dark-side-of-the-digital-humanities-part-1/ 2013

Cook, Katherine. "EmboDIYing Disruption: Queer, Feminist and Inclusive Digital Archaeologies." *European Journal of Archaeology*, vol. 22, no. 3, 2019, pp. 398–414, doi:10.1017/eaa.2019.23.

Cottom, Tressie McMillan. *Lower ed: The troubling rise of for-profit colleges in the new economy*. The New Press, 2017.

Croxall, Brian and Quinn Warnick. "Failure." *Digital Pedagogy in the Humanities - Concepts, Models, and Experiments* https://digitalpedagogy.mla.hcommons.org/keywords/failure/. 2015.

De Polignac, François. *Cults, territory, and the origins of the Greek city-state*. University of Chicago Press, 1995.

Dombrowski, Quinn. "Towards a Taxonomy of Failure." *Quinn Dombrowski*, https://www.quinndombrowski.com/?q=blog/2019/01/30/towards-taxonomy-failure. 2019

Dombrowski, Quinn. "What Ever Happened to Project Bamboo?" *Literary and Linguistic Computing*, vol. 29, no. 3, 2014, pp. 326–339, doi: 10.1093/llc/fqu026.

Epoiesen: A Journal for Creative Engagement in History and Archaeology. https://epoiesen.library.carleton.ca/.

Fitzpatrick, Kathleen. *Generous Thinking: A Radical Approach to Saving the University*. JHU Press, 2019.

Graham, Shawn, Ian Milligan, Scott Weingart. "Diversity in Digital History" themacroscope.org http://themacroscope.org/2.0/diversity-in-digital-history 2015

Hamilakis, Yannis. "Eleven Theses on the Archaeology of the Senses." *Making Sense of the Past*, edited by J. Day, Center for Archaeological Investigations, Southern Illinois University, 2013, pp. 409–419.

Leon, Sharon. "Returning Women to the History of Digital History." *6floors [bracket]*, http://www.6floors.org/bracket/2016/03/07/returning-women-to-the-history-of-digital-history/. 2016

London Charter for the Computer-Based Visualization of Cultural Heritage. 2009, http://www.londoncharter.org/.

Morrison, Aimée. "If not you then who?" *Hook and Eye* https://hookandeye.ca/2017/04/12/if-not-you-then-who/. 2017

Nowviskie, Bethany. "Two and a Half Cheers for the Lunaticks" *Bethany Nowviskie* http://nowviskie.org/2012/lunaticks/. 2012

O'Donnel, Daniel Paul. "The unessay." *Daniel Paul O'Donnell* http://people.uleth.ca/~daniel.odonnell/Teaching/the-unessay. 2012.

Owens, Trevor. "Discovery and Justification are Different: Notes on Science-ing the Humanities" *Trevor Owens*. http://www.trevorowens.org/2012/11/discovery-and-justification-are-different-notes-on-sciencing-the-humanities/. 2012.

Perry, Sara. "The Enchantment of the Archaeological Record." *European Journal of Archaeology*, vol. 1, no. 3, 2019, pp. 354–371, doi:10.1017/eaa.2019.24.

Petersen, Anne Helen. "How Millennials Became The Burnout Generation." *Buzzfeed* https://www.buzzfeednews.com/

article/annehelenpetersen/millennials-burnout-generation-debt-work. 2019

Pratchett, Terry. *Lords and Ladies* 1992; Corgi Edition 1993.

Pratchett, Terry. *Night Watch* 2002; Corgi Edition 2011.

Ramsay, Stephen. 'The Hermeneutics of Screwing Around; or What You Do with a Million Books' in K. Kee (ed) *Pastplay: Teaching and Learning History with Technology* Ann Arbor, MI: University of Michigan Press, p111-120. 2014

Ramsay, Stephen. *Reading Machines: Toward and Algorithmic Criticism*. University of Illinois Press, 2011.

Risam, Roopika. *New Digital Worlds: Postcolonial Digital Humanities in Theory, Praxis, and Pedagogy*. Northwestern University Press, 2018.

Sicart, Miguel. *The Ethics of Computer Games*. MIT press, 2011.

Van Every, Jo. "Don't do your best!" *Jo Van Every* https://jovanevery.ca/dont-do-your-best/. 2019.

Weingart, Scott. "Halting Conditions" *The Scottbot Irregular* http://www.scottbot.net/HIAL/index.html@p=12736.html. 2012

Weiss, Jules. "Guest Post: Citation is a Gift: "Punking" Accounting in #hautalk." *Footnotes* https://footnotesblog.com/2018/07/07/guest-post-citation-is-a-gift-punking-accounting-in-hautalk/. 2018.

About the Authors

Dr. Eric Kansa (PhD, Harvard University) is a digital archaeologist (with field experience the Near East, Egypt, Italy and North America) and director of Open Context (http://opencontext.org), a data publishing venue for archaeology. His research interests explore web architecture, service design and how these issues relate to the social and professional context of the digital humanities and social sciences.

Dr. Neha Gupta (PhD, McGill University) is an Assistant Professor of Anthropology at the University of British Columbia. Her research addresses geospatial and digital methods in post-colonial and Indigenous archaeology. Her research specialties are geovisualization and GIS, post-colonial and Indigenous studies, and the archaeology of India and Canada.

Dr. Shawn Graham (PhD, University of Reading) is an Associate Professor of Digital Humanities at Carleton University. His research explores bleeding-edge digital technologies in the service of archaeology, breaking them, and putting things back together in creative ways. He edits *Epoiesen, A Journal for Creative Engagement in History and Archaeology* (http://epoiesen.library.carleton.ca).